The Basketball Coaches' Complete Guide to Zone Offenses

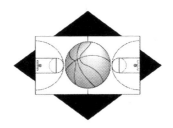

John Kimble

COACHES CHOICE™

ISBN-13: 978-1-58518-000-4
ISBN-10: 1-58518-000-9
Library of Congress Control Number: 2006933989
Book layout: Deborah Oldenburg
Cover design: Deborah Oldenburg
Front cover photo: Getty Images

Coaches Choice
P.O. Box 1828
Monterey, CA 93942
www.coacheschoice.com

Dedication

This book has taken a significant amount of time and effort to complete. Near the completion of this book, a family very close to mine suffered a tragic loss—their son, Dustin. Dustin died practicing one of his many great traits—helping others.

Sam and Sheila lost a dear son and Katie lost her loving brother. All of Dustin's friends and everyone else now live in a world that is not as decent as it was when Dustin was with us. If everyone continues to remember Dustin and to emulate just one of his many outstanding qualities such as his consideration towards other people, generosity, and compassion, then the world can slightly recover its tremendous loss.

It is for this reason that I would like to dedicate this book to Dustin Easley and his family.

—The John Kimble family

Acknowledgments

This book is dedicated to all of those who have influenced my basketball coaching life and to all the committed basketball coaches that have spent countless hours at coaching clinics, reading books, and X-ing and O-ing it with their colleagues. I have been a player, a fan, a teacher of the game, a student of the game, a coach, and a lover of the game.

As a student and a coach of the game, there have been several influences that have impacted my coaching beliefs. These influences range from summer basketball camps, coaching clinics, coaching textbooks and written publications, video tapes, observing other coaches' practices, and the countless informal coaching clinics with many other coaches trying to learn just one more drill, defense, or play. Personal influences in my coaching life have been from many of the most top-notch coaches of the game:

- The Iowa Basketball Camp (Lute Olson and Scott Thompson)
- The Doug Collins Basketball Camp (Doug Collins and Bob Sullivan)
- The University of Illinois Basketball Camp (Dick Nagy and Lou Henson)
- The Indiana Basketball Camp (Bob Knight)
- The Dick Baumgartner Shooting Camp (Dick Baumgartner)
- The Washington State University Cougar Cage Camp (George Raveling, Tom Pugliese, Mark Edwards, and Jim Livengood)
- The Snow Valley Basketball School (Herb Livesey)
- The Notre Dame University Basketball Camp (Digger Phelps and Danny Nee)
- The Illinois State University Basketball Camp (Tom Richardson)
- The Millikin University Basketball Camp (Joe Ramsey)
- Eastern Illinois University (Don Eddy)
- The Purdue University Basketball Camp (Lee Rose)
- The Oregon State University Basketball Camp (Ralph Miller and Lanny Van Eman)
- The Troy State University Basketball Camp (Don Maestri)
- The Maryville (TN) College Basketball Camp (Randy Lambert)
- The Kansas State University Basketball Camp (Jim Wooldridge, Mike Miller, Jimmy Elgas, Charles Baker, and Chad Altadonna)

Just a few of the most memorable and outstanding speakers I have heard at some of the many coaching clinics I have attended have been: Coach Lute Olson, Coach Doug Collins, Coach Hubie Brown, Coach Bob Knight, Coach Dick Nagy, Coach Don Meyers, and Coach Rick Majerus. The most outstanding authors of coaching books have been Coach Del Harris, Coach Dean Smith, Coach Bob Knight, Coach Fran Webster, Coach Lute Olson, and Coach Hubie Brown. Coach Don Meyer and Jerry Krause, Coach Del Harris, and Coach Dick Baumgartner have been authors of some of the most outstanding videotapes I have observed.

Coaching colleagues with whom I have worked are Doug Collins, Brian James, Gerry Thornton, Benny Gabbard, Steve Gould, Bob Sullivan, Norm Frazier, Tom Wierzba, Steve Laur, Ron Roher, Will Rey, Mike Davis, Dennis Kagel, Don Eiker, Bob Trimble, Dave Toler, and Ed Butkovich. I was fortunate to always be involved with tremendous coaching staffs with outstanding coaches, who were even more outstanding as people and friends to me than as coaches. The following were good friends and outstanding people: Benny Gabbard, Mitch Buckelew, Scott Huerkamp, Phil Barbara, Chris Martello, Don Tanney, Les Wilson, Al Cornish, Ron Lowery, John Lenz, Doug Zehr, and Ken Maye. To all of these people, I say thank you for your loyalty, commitment, hard work, and effort.

I would like to thank the many players I have coached as well as the extraordinary non-player students that were big parts of the basketball programs—the managers, the student statisticians, the film-takers, the student athletic trainers, and student helpers. I hope that I conveyed to each and every one of them the fact that they were important parts of the program and that they all deserve credit for the successes of their basketball programs of which they were a part.

I want to also thank the adults that I have met and become friends with in the different communities where I have coached. These are people that participated in the development and the successes of the basketball programs where I coached. These people were contributors, supporters of the program, faithful fans, and loyal friends. Some were parents of players, parents of students, and some were just fans of the game. These people are Bob and Ro Flannagan, Ed and Roseanne Moore, Ron and Mary Roher, Dick and Sharon Payne, Don and Bev Hiter, Dave Gregory, Norm Frazier, John and Pam Russell, Ken and Judy Sunderland, Fred Prager, Mark Henry, Carlan and Dee Dee Martin, George Stakely, Charles Owens, Dutch VanBuskirk, Kelly Stanford, and so many other good people.

This book is dedicated to all of those who have influenced my personal life. I was brought up by inspirational parents who always taught me to go the extra step, were always positive role models, and constant sources of encouragement and support. They taught me to never be satisfied until the job was done right. I hope I have succeeded in accomplishing that goal with the writing of this book.

My wife, Pat, was my biggest source of encouragement to write this book. She was my constant positive reinforcement and support. My daughter, Emily, and my son, Adam, also were sources of personal encouragement that helped me continue this endeavor.

My two brothers, Joe and Jim, also offered support as I slowly progressed through the ordeal of organizing and writing.

Mr. Jerry Krause (friend, coach at Gonzaga University, author, and an invaluable source of information) also was of great help and encouragement, as was Mr. Murray Pool (former high school coach and current publisher of *Basketball Sense*, friend, and source of information).

Gerry Thornton, longtime friend and fellow student of the game, has affected my coaching career probably more than any other person, while Benny Gabbard was the one person who got me started in my junior college coaching career and showed great faith and confidence in me in my first years of coaching junior college basketball.

I also wish to thank Mr. Mike Willard who converted all of my many hand-drawn diagrams into computer-generated works of professional art.

This book is dedicated to all of those students of the game who have the same love and passion for basketball as I have always had.

Contents

Dedication 3

Acknowledgments 4

Foreword 8

Introduction 9

Chapter 1: Zone Offense Concepts 11

Chapter 2: The Beginnings of Attacking a Zone Defense– 27
Primary and Secondary Break and Half-Court Situations

Chapter 3: The Baseline Zone Continuity Offense, ... 39
the Pin-Screen Zone Continuity Offense, the 2 Slide Zone
Continuity Offense, and the Corners Trap Offense

Chapter 4: The Diamond Zone Continuity Offense 60

Chapter 5: The Heavy and Rotation Zone Continuity Offenses 81

Chapter 6: The Triple-Post Zone Continuity Offense. 111

Chapter 7: Breakdown Drills 128

Chapter 8: The Corners Trap Offense 170

About the Author 196

Foreword

We have known Coach John Kimble for close to 30 years. Not only did Brian James play American Legion Baseball under his leadership, but we watched his basketball teams win consistently year after year. Most observers have always felt that much of John's success was due to the fact of his total preparation. Getting teams ready to play to the best of their ability physically and mentally is not easy to do by any means. This attribute has always been one of John's strongest. His preparation for even minute details often was a deciding factor in coming out on top in close games. When John would work with us at the Doug Collins Basketball Camp held at Concordia University in River Forest, Illinois, we would sit night after night of each week of camp for 10 summers talking basketball with all of the coaches. John would always be in the middle of discussions about basketball situations, either talking or listening and learning. We felt that we had some of the top high school and college coaches in the Midwest working with us at that time. Coach Kimble's preparation of this book shows those same characteristics with many details given for each and every zone offense described.

Having great zone offenses that can attack any type of zone defense is imperative in today's game. By reading Coach Kimble's book on zone attacks, any coach can begin to understand the importance of keeping the ball moving, penetrating and pitching to an open man, flashing to open areas, effective screening, offensive perimeter players getting their feet set, overloading one side of the floor, sealing for position, giving your teammate a good pass, and so forth. We work on these things every day in practice. At the NBA level, zone defenses have become legal (as long as a team doesn't have a defender standing in the lane without being able to touch any opponent every 2.9 seconds) and also have a 24-second shot clock for the offensive team. We found this book to be a great teaching tool for us personally, simply because NBA coaches have never had to worry about teams playing zone defenses. Now since zone defenses are somewhat legal in the NBA, NBA coaches are scurrying about, getting all of their old clinic notes out from their earlier coaching days from high school or college. We are also trying to watch tapes or sit with coaches with zone offensive or zone defensive success. We have done all of that, but we can honestly say that we got just as much insight and recall on how to attack the zone defense from Coach John Kimble's book than we did sitting in any coaching session or reading any other book on the shelves today. This book truly is a coach's delight.

–Doug Collins
Former Head Coach
Washington Wizards

–Brian James
Assistant Coach
Milwaukee Bucks

Introduction

The purpose for writing this book is to help basketball coaches develop their entire zone offense package and impact the philosophy on successful methods of attacking zone defenses, the specific zone offenses utilized, alignments/sets that are used, plays and entries that are run, and drills that are used to improve players' skills and performance levels.

The first chapter helps the reader develop, modify, or expand his concepts and methods of how to attack zone defenses. I have given each concept a number. These numbers will be displayed throughout the book in the following form: (16). This symbol means concept 16 needs to be referred to if you are going to fully understand the slide, the technique, the drill, or the axiom involved in attacking the zone.

The second chapter offers the beginnings of the zone attack, namely the fast break and the secondary break. I also include the out-of-bounds plays from the sideline and the baseline. These flow into the beginning alignments of the zone offenses. Also, our exact program of attack is given in a philosophy section.

Chapters 3, 4, 5, and 6 are broken into zone continuities. They are presented from a set platform. For example, Chapter 3 gives our four basic continuities from the 2-3 set; Chapter 4, the 1-2-2 set; Chapter 5, the 1-3-1 set; and Chapter 6, the 2-1-2 overload set. Not only are the continuities offered, but also different entries into each of the continuities. These entries display dribbling as well as passing entries and breakdown drills specific to those particular continuities conclude the chapters.

Chapter 7 is a complete chapter on breakdown drills for fundamentals and for general zone attacks. From the specific breakdown drills in the four chapters on continuities and the general breakdown drills of Chapter 7, coaches should be able to work up a drill package that will improve their zone attack, your teams offensive fundamentals, and teach and re-teach the cuts and movements of your chosen continuities.

Chapter 8 displays our method of attacking pressure zones. You can easily note that this attack is also a continuity that flows into the positions of the other continuities.

When you are through reading this book, you should have the basic philosophy of attack: fast break into secondary break into continuity (with many different dribbling and passing entries into each continuity). Also, you can easily see the basic three principles evolve: same entry, different set; different entries, same set; and different entries, different sets. These options gives you a multiple attack and you only have to incorporate what you think your personnel for that specific year can handle.

Coaches should understand that with a little extra effort and creativity, some of the zone offenses can be integrated to form a hybrid combination of two offenses to provide that enterprising coach with an even more lethal zone offensive attack. These combinations must first be thoroughly learned and evaluated before deciding to make such a decision of combining two zone offenses. A coaching staff can utilize this book to use different zone offenses every season that will be appropriate and fit that specific team's talent-level and skill limitations.

Coaches must also understand that although the entire book should be read and analyzed, only one, two, or three (at the most) zone offenses should be chosen for that season's use. So, the coaching staff must gain a thorough understanding of all the zone offenses explained before making a commitment to the correct zone offense for the personnel of that season's team. Coaches should also realize that other alignments/sets, other entries, and other breakdown drills that the staff can create on their own can fit into the particular zone offense and are encouraged to fit that particular team's needs and wants.

1

Zone Offense Concepts

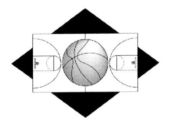

Many coaches believe in the man-to-man defense, while others value the half-court pressure in the form of zone traps, as well as different versions of man-to-man double-team pressure that can be incorporated. Still, a great deal of coaches believe in the half-court zone defense. Zone defense coaches have a significant arsenal from the various zone defenses that exist. They range from the different types of match-up zones, box-and-one zones, triangle-and-two zones, 1-2-2 zones, 1-1-3 zones, 1-3-1 zones, 2-1-2 zones, or 2-3 zones. All of these defenses have their place in basketball and all have their own particular strengths (as well as their weaknesses). Successful offensive-minded coaches must have within their offensive repertoire the concepts of how to attack the various zone defenses that their teams could eventually face during the course of a season. A successful offensive-minded coach cannot have a different zone offense for each and every zone defense that exists, but he can research and develop a zone offense concept package. This package could be a building block for all of the zone offenses that his teams will use.

Zone Offense Concepts

Concept 1: Utilize a primary and secondary fast break system that is compatible with, and that fully complements, your zone offense package.

By using a primary and a secondary fast break, you have more opportunities to beat the opponent's defense in transition, thereby gaining a numerical advantage, or at least an organizational advantage, for the offense. Think of primary and secondary fast breaks as a faster-paced entry into the zone offense continuity that you are using (Diagrams 1.1 and 1.2).

Diagram 1.1 displays the end of the fast break. O1 is the ball handler and O2 and O3 are the two outside lane fillers. O4 moves down the center lane, cutting into a low post position. O5 is the trailer, who positions himself for the outside shot should all the other options fail. If O5 is an adequate three-point shooter, he could station himself outside the three-point arc.

Diagram 1.2 shows the secondary part of the fast break. When the initial thrust fails, O1 reverses the ball by passing to O5 who passes to O3. Meanwhile, O4 has timed his move to the opposite low post block to coincide with O3's receiving of the ball. O2 has cut along the baseline and moved up the lane to set a back screen for O5. O5 dips and cuts off O2's screen for a lob pass from O3. If this move fails, O2 replaces O5 at the top of the key and O1 remains at the weakside wing. The team is now in a position to continue their zone attack from a 1-2-2 formation, with O3 and O1 at the two wing locations, O2 at the top of the key, and O4 and O5 at the two low post areas. See Chapter 2 for more on the primary and secondary fast break, which complements your zone offense.

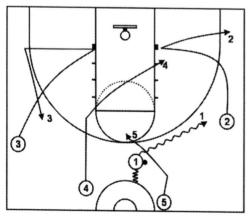

Diagram 1.1

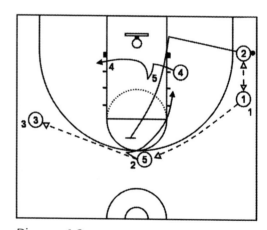

Diagram 1.2

Concept 2: Use different sets/alignments and entries/plays to be more varied and less predictable to opposing defenses.

Various sets and entries can be used to become less predictable to the opposition while still maintaining a degree of simplicity for your own team. Diagrams 1.3 through 1.8 exhibit offensive zone spot-up locations. With minimum player adjustment, all six sets begin where the secondary break ends, allowing the offense to stay on the attack and not give the defense any re-set time. In Diagram 1.3, all players are in the same position where the secondary break ends. This play is called diamond continuity spot-ups, which is described in detail in Chapter 4.

In Diagram 1.4, O4 cuts across the lane to post up while O5 steps out to the short corner to set the offense. This move is done while O3 passes the ball back to O1. Then, zone offense continuity begins. This play is called heavy continuity, which is described in detail in Chapter 5.

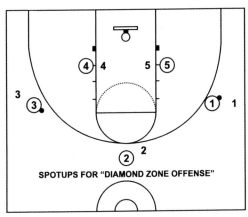

Diagram 1.3

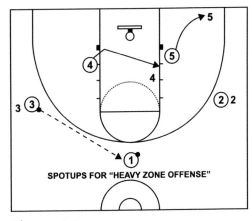

Diagram 1.4

The same is true for Diagram 1.5, in which O4 cuts to the medium post area (this play is called rotation continuity, described in Chapter 5) and when the ball is at the top of the key, O5 pops out to the deep corner. In Diagram 1.6, O4 cuts to the high post from the secondary break's ending positions (again, the rotation continuity) and O5 pops out to the deep corner.

In Diagram 1.7, O3 can pass the ball back out to O2 and then cut to the baseline with O1 rotating up. The four zone offenses (baseline, pin screen, 2 slide, and corner continuities, described in Chapter 3) are ready to continue without having to re-set.

In Diagram 1.8, both post players, O4 and O5, break to the high post. This play is a variation of the diamond continuity (described in detail in Chapter 4).

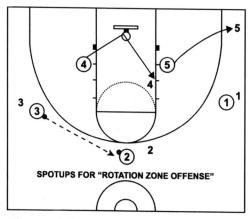

Diagram 1.5

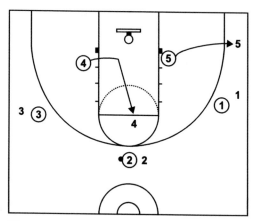

Diagram 1.6

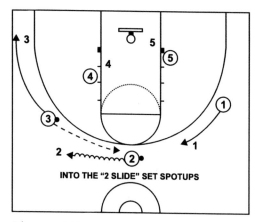

Diagram 1.7

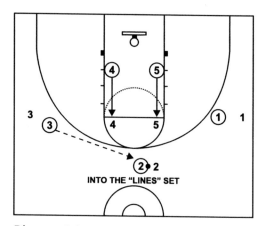

Diagram 1.8

Concept 3: Every zone defense has inherent weaknesses.

Get to know the particular styles of the zone defense that is being used by your opponents (the basic slides and responsibilities in that zone) so that you may attack and capitalize on the weaknesses of each defense.

Concept 4: Capitalize on the strengths of the offensive alignment/set by distorting the shape of the original zone defense.

To capitalize on the offensive alignment's strengths, use different entries. This strategy can include using stacks, overloads, odd front offensive sets versus even front zone defenses, even front offensive alignments versus odd front zone defenses, or unique and unconventional-looking alignments.

Concept 5: Having a zone offense continuity with clearly defined responsibilities and assignments can create levels of specialization that will showcase individual player's talent levels and improve the overall effectiveness of the zone offense.

This concept allows the coach to adjust his zone offense to accommodate the specific and unique talent on his current ball club. A great shooter, for example, can be placed in a position to better use his shooting abilities. The best rebounders should be located near the basket to better capitalize on their specific strengths. The best ball handlers should be positioned so that they can utilize their dribbling skills.

Concept 6: Capitalize on your offensive personnel's individual strengths via various entries/plays or different alignments/sets.

Certain offensive alignments or sets can give specific individual offensive players added advantages of being able to use their strengths within the offense. Entries or plays can also allow offensive individuals opportunities to highlight their talents.

Concept 7: Use different entries and/or alignments to capitalize on an opposing individual's defensive weaknesses.

Certain offensive alignments or sets can exploit individual defender's weaknesses. However, a coaching staff must analyze and discover those weaknesses and then incorporate specific entries or sets to attack those weaknesses.

Concept 8: Make sure that defensive transition responsibilities (i.e., preventing opponents from getting into their fast break offense) are clear-cut and carried out by all five players in the zone offense.

Not only should it be clearly defined who gets back, but what getting back really means: how far back and where. Assign one player as your "tailback," who is your defensive safety. He is to get his "tail back" on any loss of possession of the ball. Upon recognition that your opponent has obtained possession of the basketball, your "tailback" quickly sprints to the center jump circle. This depth and central location allows that "tailback" to be able to defend your basket from either the left or the right side of the opposition's transition attack. Also, assign one of the smaller rebounders to become the "halfback"—in other words, "half" offensive rebounder and "half" defensive safety. This "halfback" should initially locate around the free throw line. From this position, the "halfback" can more quickly charge the offensive boards or drop to defend, whichever is needed at that moment. The three best rebounders are designated as the three "fullbacks." Their "full" responsibility is to attack the offensive boards.

Concept 9: Have clear-cut offensive rebounding responsibility rules for all five players in the zone offense and make sure that they are executed by every player in the zone offense.

With every shot, emphasize the importance of overloading the weakside rebounding areas. Constantly emphasize to your players that there should be a distinct offensive rebounding advantage when going against zone defenses. Assign three players as your "fullbacks" (your main offensive rebounders), one as your "halfback" (your half rebounder), and one as your "tailback" (your defensive safety). In general, you should have at least three-and-a-half offensive rebounders attacking the weakside area for offensive rebounding purposes. Diagram 1.9 shows a typical movement from an offensive set into offensive rebounding and defensive floor balance positioning.

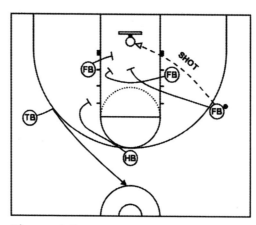

Diagram 1.9

Concept 10: Reverse the ball to force the defensive zone to defend both sides of the floor.

Reversing the ball makes every zone defender move and shift. This technique forces the opposition to think and move when they assume new defensive responsibilities and areas on the court. In addition, quick ball-reversals can fatigue a zone defense, and also place the ball in designated spots before the defense can arrive at that spot.

Concept 11: Maintain good floor balance and spacing in the zone offense.

It is good to have 15 to 18 feet between all of the players. This spacing forces the defense to stretch out to cover a larger area, thus possibly weakening it. Having good floor balance makes the concept even more of an offensive threat.

Concept 12: Zone offensive players should know the value of the dribble and utilize the dribble properly. Utilize the various dribbles in the zone offenses.

Perimeter players should remember to value the importance of the dribble. Zone offense players should not waste their dribble, but should use it wisely. Players with the ball should always be in a triple-threat position. Perimeter players should not pass the ball too quickly. It is better to be too slow than too quick. Perimeter players should give offensive cutters (interior and exterior) enough time to get open. Remember that a player cannot score or make the assist if he has already given up the possession of the ball by passing the ball too soon. Passers should pass over or around the defense—not through the defense. Passes should be made away from the defender and not just to the offensive teammate.

In zone offenses, use the dribble to advance the ball to the basket, to improve the passing angles (down dribbles), to get out of defensive traps, to force two defenders on the ball (gap dribbles or freeze dribbles), to increase confusion of the zone defense, or to pull zone defenders away from their assigned defensive area (pull dribbles). Post players should never dribble with their back to the basket without first looking at the basket.

Down Dribbles

Utilize down dribbles in zone offenses to flatten out zone defenses. Down dribbles are dribbles down to a baseline with the idea of a quick ball reversal to beat the zone defense's reaction on the opposite side of the floor, or to improve the passing angle to a post player on the same side of the floor (Diagram 1.10).

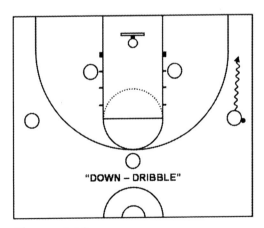

"DOWN – DRIBBLE"

Diagram 1.10

Gap Dribbles

Gap dribbles should be used for penetration into seams (or gaps) of the zone defense's perimeter to force two defenders onto one offensive player. Remember to emphasize to all gap dribblers the importance of momentarily retaining the dribble when they initially gap dribble, so if the defensive pressure is too great, the dribblers can always back out away from the defense (Diagram 1.11).

Pull Dribbles

Pull dribbles are dribbles on the perimeter to pull a zone perimeter defender out of his protective area, which weakens that specific area of the defense. The weakened area should then be attacked. Pull-dribble-and-replace is a solid offensive theory to use against zone defenses. This theory is simply pulling one zone defender out of his area via the dribble, while having another offensive man step into that vacated area, looking for a throw-back pass from the pull dribbler. In Diagram 1.12, O3 pull dribbles out into the wing area that O2 has vacated (after he passed the ball to O3 and cut through the zone defense). O5 replaces O3 in the short-corner area where O3 previously was. O4 gap-cuts into the area that O5 has just vacated as O5 replaces O3 in his initial area.

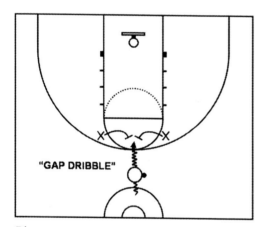

Diagram 1.11

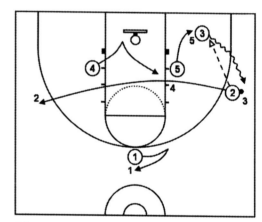

Diagram 1.12

Freeze Dribbles

Freeze dribbles are used on the perimeter to pull one or more perimeter zone defenders out of their protective areas. A freeze dribble is when an offensive player dribbles directly at a particular perimeter zone defender to freeze him; then, the defender can do nothing but take on the dribbler. When you freeze dribble the next-to-nearest defender, you have also incorporated a pull dribble on the nearest defender and a freeze dribble on the next-closest zone defender. Diagram 1.13 illustrates O1 freeze dribbling at X2 while pull dribbling X1. This technique puts tremendous pressure on X4. Does he step up to guard O3? If so, who picks up O5 (on his gap cut) and who picks up O4 (on his gap cut)? This strategy creates a great deal of confusion for the zone defenders, and, therefore, places a significant amount of pressure on the defense.

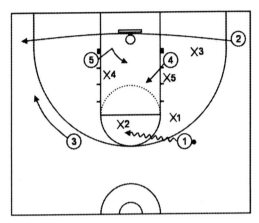

Diagram 1.13

Concept 13: When catching the basketball, zone offensive players should be prepared to become immediate offensive threats as shooters, passers, or dribblers.

When a perimeter player is anticipating receiving a pass on the perimeter, he should always have his feet and hands ready. Coaches should emphasize many different techniques by constantly using the following phrases:

- "Get behind the ball."

- "Have your inside pivot foot already planted and pointed toward the basket, with your hands up, ready to catch and shoot quickly."

- "Make your teammates better passers by giving them a catcher's mitt target, with the palm of your shooting hand already pointing toward the ball and your guide hand already on the side."

- "Know where you are in relation to the three-point line. If you want to take a three-point shot, get behind the three-point line before you catch the ball. As you catch the ball, you can step up to the line, creating momentum toward the basket and, therefore, a longer shooting range."

Coaches should look for the details of these techniques. All of these phrases should be used on a daily basis in the evaluation of the players' execution of the techniques. These fundamental techniques are valuable aspects for a player to be successful. These techniques should be critiqued and stressed in breakdown drills, scrimmages, and games. Constructive criticism as well as positive reinforcement should be given at many different times in practices as well as in games.

Concept 14: Zone offensive players should remember the value of ball fakes and shot fakes.

Fakes are particularly effective because zone defenses are very much ball-oriented. The basketball attracts the majority of each defender's attention. Zone offenses should use that fact to their advantage and utilize both types of fakes. This use of fakes forces individual zone defenders to move and to react more, which can physically (and mentally) wear down defenders. The use of ball fakes compels the defense to move without the ball moving, thereby creating openings in the slides of the zone defense. This approach helps make the zone defense weaker and easier to attack.

Concept 15: Zone offensive players should utilize skip passes.

Perimeter players should know and take advantage of the importance of skip passes. Be sure to have your players practice both throwing and catching skip passes during every practice. In zone offenses, it is good to remember that one good skip pass deserves another. After using a pull dribble and then a skip pass, the offense could have an open perimeter shot. If not, it is probably because the zone defense has reacted well to the first skip pass. A second skip pass can then be extra effective. An additional benefit is that successfully utilizing a second skip pass discourages a defensive team from hustling and reacting to the initial skip pass.

Concept 16: Attack the zone defense from behind.

Defenders cannot defend an offensive player they cannot see. Remember that all zones are ball-oriented; their primary attention is to the basketball. So, if an offensive player

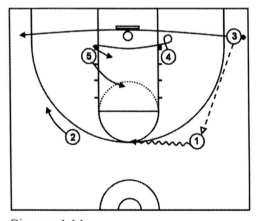

Diagram 1.14

without the ball hides out behind the defense, he could be forgotten and therefore will not be defended. Diagram 1.14 illustrates O3, O4, and O5 attacking the zone from behind. All three players attempt to stay behind all five of the zone defenders, as the ball is being reversed out on top attracts most of the attention of the zone defense. All three players should have excellent opportunities to get open near the basket.

Concept 17: Flatten the zone defense by getting the basketball down to the baseline and then reverse the ball quickly to the opposite side of the floor.

Place the ball on the baseline on one side of the defense and flatten out the zone before quickly reversing the basketball to the other side. All zone defenses become a 2-3 zone alignment when flattened. Regardless of the initial defensive alignment the offense faces, the offense knows where each defender will be when the ball reaches the corner. Trying to beat the reaction of the zone defense can be an effective method of defeating zone defenses. Down-passes, down-dribbles, or skip passes are the only ways to get the ball down to the corner and should be utilized often (Diagrams 1.15 and 1.16). Diagram 1.15 illustrates a down pass while Diagram 1.16 demonstrates a down dribble. Both are primary methods of getting the ball to the corner, thereby flattening the zone.

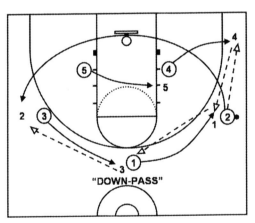

"DOWN-PASS"

Diagram 1.15

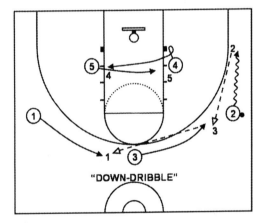

"DOWN-DRIBBLE"

Diagram 1.16

Concept 18: Screen defenders in the zone defense with on-the-ball screens and/or off-the-ball screens.

Use on-the-ball screens with the screener rolling to the basket and posting up (Diagram 1.17). Other times, you could utilize a ball screen with the screener stepping out on the perimeter after setting the screen (called slipping the screen), or with the screener flaring out on the perimeter (Diagram 1.18).

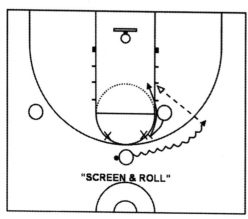

"SCREEN & ROLL"

Diagram 1.17

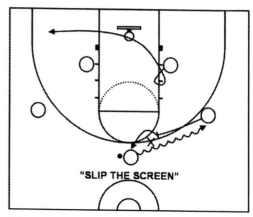

"SLIP THE SCREEN"

Diagram 1.18

Off-the-ball screens could be used as pin screens to pin the perimeter defender in, particularly on the baseline. Screens coming from or taking place in the interior of the zone can also be very effective. In Diagram 1.19, O1 can reverse the ball to O2 who passes to O3, coming off the pin screens of O4 and O5; or, O1 can "skip pass" to O3 by skipping O2 in the reversal.

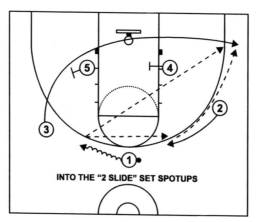

INTO THE "2 SLIDE" SET SPOTUPS

Diagram 1.19

Concept 19: Using cutters (from the perimeter who cut through the heart of the zone defense to the opposite side of the offense) is another effective method of attacking zone defenses.

In Diagram 1.20, O2 passes to O5 and cuts while O1 replaces O2, completing the cut and replace technique. Note that the down pass created a flattened zone defense. The theory of cut and replace in Diagram 1.20 is also very effective, while the theory of dribble and replace can also be very instrumental in the success of a zone offense, as shown in Diagram 1.21, in which O1 flare-cuts to the weakside wing, causing O2 to replace O1 at the top of the key. This move opens up the ballside wing area for O3. O3 dribbles outside while O5 replaces O3. O5 "attacks" the zone from behind by cutting and replacing the vacant spot left open by O3's dribbling out to the wing.

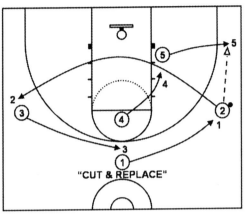

Diagram 1.20

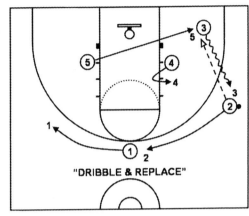

Diagram 1.21

Concept 20: Anytime the ball is passed into the middle of a zone defense, the receiver should look to extend the pass to a player closer to the basket and on the opposite side of the floor from where the original pass originated.

Versus full-court or half-court zone-trap pressure, when the ball is passed into the middle, look to extend the pass; in other words, have the player look over his weakside shoulder first and look to make the pass in that direction. In Diagram 1.22, O2 passes inside to O4, who turns to find a teammate, O5, breaking to the low block on the weakside.

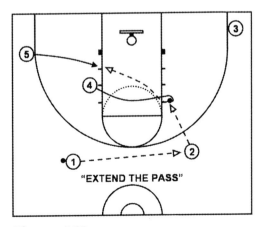

Diagram 1.22

Concept 21: If the ball is passed inside to a post player, perimeter players should flare-cut to the various soft spots in the zone defense and be prepared to quickly catch and shoot off of the pass.

If the ball is passed inside to a post player, all perimeter players should look for the closest open area on the perimeter (especially on the weakside, away from the post player with the ball) and cut to that area. These movements are called flare-cuts. The perimeter players do not have any *exact* spots they should go to on their flare-cuts, just anywhere with an opening. In Diagram 1.23, O2 has passed inside to O4. O1, O2, and O3 all execute flare-cuts to find openings around the perimeter for a pass back out from O4.

Concept 22: Post players should gap-cut in the middle of the zone defense.

Interior players who flash in the post area should gap-cut; that is, they should flash in the post area that is free of zone defenders—the gap of the defense. These gaps are not pre-designated or predictable on their location, rather, these gaps are created by the many slides of the zone defense. Diagram 1.24 illustrates gap cuts by both O4 and O5.

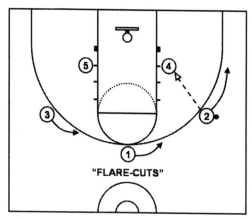

"FLARE-CUTS"

Diagram 1.23

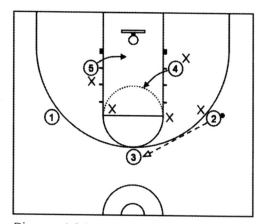

Diagram 1.24

Concept 23: When passing the ball to offensive post players, perimeter players should use bounce-passes away from the post defenders (unless it is a lob pass to a player behind the zone).

If your post players are fronted, lob the ball away from the fronting defender at a pre-designated spot (use the ballside corner of the backboard, since it is a consistent target for all passers and receivers). If the defense is playing on the low side of the offensive post player, the passer should pass the ball away from the defense on the high side of the post player. If the defense is playing on the high side of the offensive post player, the passer should pass the ball away from the defense on the low side of the post player. If the defense is fronting the offensive post, the perimeter passer should throw the ball away from the fronting defense toward the basket. As in perimeter passing, make all passes to post players away from the defense and not just towards the offensive player.

Concept 24: Offensive post players should look to obtain (and then maintain) body position advantages over their post defenders.

For instance, if the post defender plays the post on the high side, that offensive player should set up even higher in the lane (to give himself additional room for a pass made on the low side). If the post defense plays your post player on the low side, your offensive player should set up even lower (to give himself more room for a pass made on the high side). This creation of space by the post player could compel other defenders to help on the opening of inside space, thereby creating extra opportunities for perimeter players.

Concept 25: Post players should know and effectively implement specific offensive post moves after catching the ball in the zone defense's interior.

Whenever possible, post players who catch the ball in the post area should hop and land on both feet simultaneously as the ball is being caught. This technique enables the offensive post player to use either foot as a pivot foot and leave either opposite foot as the free foot. The ball should be firmly placed under the chin as the post player looks over his high shoulder to locate the defense. A power drop-step move (away from the defense) and an appropriate power move should then be made. If the post defender has overplayed a particular side of the offensive post player, the offensive post player should attack the opposite side. If the defender has not fully committed to a specific side, the offensive post player should attack the defender and force a decision before attacking the opposite side again. Have your players use the show-and-go-opposite move, the square-up and up-and-under moves, and the whirl move. All of these moves should be practiced daily with different variations at the end of the move. At the end of these three basic moves, players should end up with no shot-fakes, one shot-fake, and two shot-fakes.

The show-and-go-opposite offensive post move is executed by the post player first hopping (with both feet) as he catches the ball and immediately chinning the ball. He should then look over his top shoulder (the shoulder away from the baseline). He then will see any perimeter defenders dropping down to double-team. Oftentimes, the offensive post player will feel the post defender making physical contact with him on either the low side or the high side. By looking over his top shoulder, he could also see the post defender that has declared the high side as the side he wants to overplay. If he sees the defenders, he shows the ball to the defender by partially bringing the ball up toward the top shoulder and immediately using the low foot (foot nearest the baseline) to drop-step and seal off the defender. If the offensive post player hops and chins, looks over his top shoulder and doesn't see the post defender, he can show the ball toward the low shoulder before drop-stepping with his top foot and sealing off the defender on the high side. If the offensive post player sees perimeter defenders collapsing, he should quickly kick the ball out to a perimeter player located in the area where the double-down defender is coming from.

The square-up and up-and-under moves should primarily be used when the offensive post player cannot see or feel the overplay by the post defender. The offensive post player simply pivots and faces the basket and the defender, instantly becoming an attacking threat to the defense. One simple shot fake often causes the defender to react to the fake. The post player then ducks under the arms of the defender to either drive to the basket or to take the shot. This move often draws defensive fouls and puts opposing post defenders in quick foul trouble.

The whirl move (sometimes called the Hakeem Olajuwon move) is another form of aggressive attack on the post defender by approaching the basket on the side away from the defender. However, instead of sealing off the defender with his legs, butt, and back, the offensive player seals off the defender with the legs and chest. This technique is done in the following manner. For example, if the post player feels and sees the opposition over-playing him on the high side, the offensive player pivots off of the low foot and whirls around toward the low side (away from the defender). He seals the defender off with his legs and chest as he dribble attacks to the basket.

When the defense is playing behind post players, post players should use the duck-in move and be ready to then use either a power move or a face-up move. The spin-and-post-up move should be implemented by offensive post players when the defense is fronting the duck-in move.

Concept 26: Patient and continuous zone offenses can become effective defenses as well as efficient and productive offenses.

Zone offenses must be patient and move the ball, as well as offensive personnel, forcing the defensive personnel to move. Remember, *they* cannot score if *you* have the ball.

Particularly against non-trapping zone defenses, the offensive team should be able to dictate who takes the shot, the type and the location of the shot, and when they take the shot. Zone offenses should utilize the opportunity of controlling the tempo and limiting the number of offensive possessions of the opponent while maximizing the quality of their own shot selection. Making both your offense and defense more effective will greatly increase your team's chances of winning.

2

The Beginnings of Attacking a Zone Defense— Primary and Secondary Break and Half-Court Situations

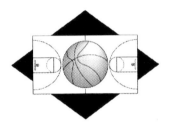

The zone offensive philosophy presented in this book consists of a primary fast break, which leads into a secondary fast break, which leads into a zone continuity offense at the full-court level. From the half-court level, the offense starts with a zone offense entry/play and flows into the zone offense continuity. The movement from one phase to the next should not result in having to reset. One phase should flow smoothly to the next. After one phase has been completed, the players are in position to begin the next phase, thereby denying the defense any time to regroup.

Primary Fast Break

The primary fast break is used to apply constant pressure on the opponents' defenses as well as to beat the opposition down the floor to provide your offense with high percentage shots and good rebounding opportunities. The primary fast break must be run to either side of the floor. Limiting your primary break to just the right side of the floor severely handicaps your offense. Just as you want to make sure that a right-handed

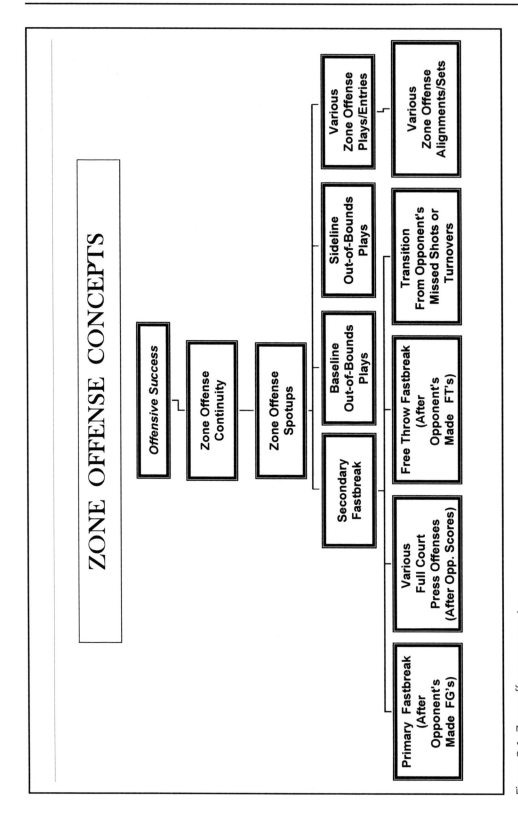

Figure 2.1. Zone offense concepts

point guard can go to his left, your primary fast break should be an ambidextrous break. A particular primary break could be run after opponents have scored a free throw, while another primary fast break could be run on any and all other situations. This break could be the same as the made or missed field goal primary break. A primary break can be implemented:

- after opponents' turnovers.
- after opponents' missed field goal shots.
- after opponents' made shots.
- after opponents' made free throws (a different primary break could be used on opponents' missed free throws).

Diagrams 2.1 and 2.2 display the end of the primary. O1 is the point guard. He dribbles the ball with a speed dribble down the middle of the floor while O2 and O3 (the wings) race down the outside lanes all the way to the free throw lane. This play is the three-man fast break, which will lead to lay-ups. O4 comes down the middle lane, and when he gets to the free throw line extended opposite of O1, he cuts across the lane to the new ballside low post for a possible pass from O1 and a post-up move inside. You can call this maneuver the beginning of the secondary break or the end of the primary break. O5, the safety, follows down the middle lane. As O1 dribbles to clear the middle lane, O5 stations himself just outside the three-point arc, centered for a possible pass from O1 for the three-point shot (Diagrams 2.1 and 2.2).

Diagram 2.1 shows the attack to the left side of the floor and Diagram 2.2 exhibits the attack to the right side of the floor. From this point on, for the sake of brevity, all options will be shown only from the right side of the floor.

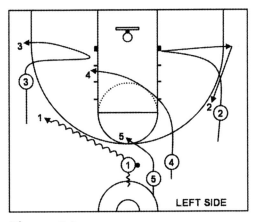

Diagram 2.1

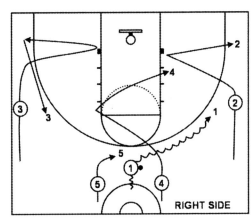

Diagram 2.2

Secondary Fast Break

The secondary fast break flows directly from the primary fast break or from a press offense against a full-court zone or man-to-man press. The secondary break is used to continue the offensive pressure placed on the opposing defenses. It is used to provide your offense with a numerical advantage, if not an organizational advantage. Again, it is extremely important that the secondary break be comfortably run to both the left and the right side of the floor (Diagrams 2.1 and 2.2). Note that Diagram 1.1 is exactly like Diagram 2.2. This play is Concept 1 in the zone offense. Relevant concept numbers will be noted in parentheses in the book (#1) so you can see how the concepts actually occur in the zone offenses.

Diagram 2.3 shows the second phase of the secondary break with minor adjustments to take advantage of specific skills of different players in different years (#6). In Diagram 1.2, Chapter 1, O2 broke along the baseline and provided a back screen for O5 and a lob pass from O3. This move was the first option of the secondary break. Meanwhile, O4 gap cuts to an inside opening on the new ball side (#22). Notice in Diagram 2.3 that the ball had been taken to the corner to O2 before being passed back out to O1, who reversed it to O5 and then to O3, who cut up from the corner on the primary fast break (#10, #11, #13, #17, #18, #19, #22, #24, #26).

Diagram 2.3 offers an option from the secondary break shown in Diagram 2.2 (and Diagram 1.2) (#6). In Diagram 2.3, O5 sets a diagonal down screen for O2 to break outside the three-point arc for a three-point shot. O4 breaks across the lane, searching for an inside pass from O5 and O3. So in years when a team has a big athlete type player at O5, Diagram 1.2 is best for the second phase of the break. However, in years when a team has exceptional outside three-point shooters at the O2 and O3 positions, Diagram 2.3 is best (#6). This difference illustrates how small adjustments can be made to take advantage of specific skills of current players (#6).

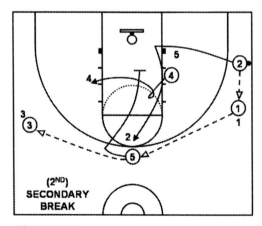

Diagram 2.3

Diagram 2.4 offers the third and final phase of the secondary break. Regardless of which option a team runs in the second phase, players will be in the same position for the third phase. In this final phase, O4 can receive an inside pass on a lob pass from O3. If the ball is reversed to O2, O4 could receive a bounce pass from O2 on O4's duck-in cut. If not open because O4 is aggressively defended, O5 screens across the lane for O4 as the ball is reversed from O3 to O2. After screening for O4, O5 can cut up the lane to a gap in the zone, should one become available.

Diagram 2.5 offers another variation on the double screen set by O4 and O5 for O2 in Diagram 2.3. In Diagram 2.5, after O1 has passed to O5 and O5 has passed to O3, O1 and O5 set the staggered double screen for the great shooter, O2. Staggered double screens are much harder for the defenders to defend. O1 sets the first screen and O5 sets the second screen several feet away from O1's screen. Switching defenses have massive trouble with this type of screening. This move could free O2 for the three-point shot while O4 cuts to the open gap inside the defense (#6, #7, #8, #13#16, #17, #18, #19, #22, #26).

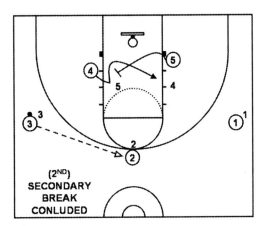

Diagram 2.4

Diagram 2.5

The secondary break option(s) could vary from year to year, depending on the team's strengths and weaknesses. If a team can mentally handle it, you could have more than one secondary break. The variation of the secondary fast break could be after the ball is reversed from the deep corner, or it could be an even more dramatic difference. The use of a particular break could depend upon what the opposition has just done with the basketball. For instance, if the opposing offense just scored a three-pointer, a pre-determined secondary break could be used for just that particular situation (the difference between Diagram 2.3 and Diagram 2.5).

Running multiple primary and/or secondary fast breaks gives the offensive team the obvious advantage of using the strengths of specific offensive individuals, as well as being much less scoutable and predictable to the opposition. Your team could use one secondary break against all zone defenses, while a different secondary break could be used against all man-to-man defenses. Or, a specific secondary break could be run only when the ball is on one designated side of the floor, with a different secondary break being run on the opposite side of the court. The number and types of secondary breaks could (and should) depend on your team's capabilities—physically and mentally—from year to year (#6).

Zone Offense Spot-Up Positions

Before beginning an explanation of all the different zone sets, spot-up positions need to be explored. These spot-up positions are easily recognizable as each set is explained.

Zone offense spot-up positions are the designated positions on the floor that are advantageous in achieving good shot selection, rebounding opportunities, offensive floor balance, and defensive transition availabilities. Diagram 2.6 shows the spot-up locations of the baseline zone offense, the 2 slide, and the pin-screen continuity offense (Chapter 3). Diagram 2.7 shows the spot-ups of the diamond zone offense (Chapter 4). Diagram 2.8 shows the spot-ups of the heavy zone offense (Chapter 5). The rotation zone offense's spot-ups are illustrated in Diagram 2.9 (Chapter 5). All spot-ups can be used with the ball being on either side of the floor.

Individual Specialization for Players

Specialization is an integral part of your zone offense that is used to more fully take advantage of individual strengths and to minimize individual players' weaknesses. With repetition in practice (as well as in games), players can more easily develop the specific skills needed to be successful in the zone offense (#5, #6).

As your post players concentrate their time and energy on their inside game, they become more proficient and effective in that aspect of the game. Your perimeter players work on the little things that make their outside game better. Mix your post and perimeter some, so that all of your players are well rounded (both as post players and as perimeter players), but remember that your zone offense is a little more specialized. This focus should make the offense more efficient, more effective, more productive, and, therefore, more successful.

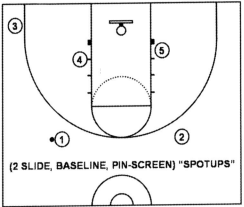

(2 SLIDE, BASELINE, PIN-SCREEN) "SPOTUPS"

Diagram 2.6

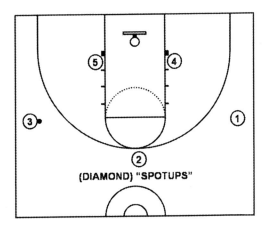

(DIAMOND) "SPOTUPS"

Diagram 2.7

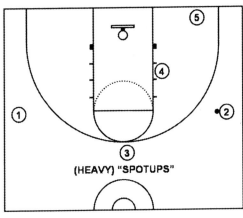

(HEAVY) "SPOTUPS"

Diagram 2.8

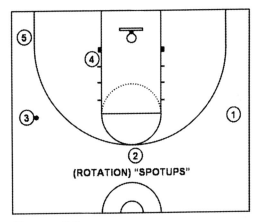

(ROTATION) "SPOTUPS"

Diagram 2.9

Ruled Continuity Patterns

A ruled zone offense continuity pattern, which can consist of just a few simple rules, allows the offense to be run for indefinite periods of time. The zone offense continuity allows for fluid movement, good shot opportunities, good floor balance, and good defensive transition capabilities. The continuity is run out of the spot-ups for a limitless period of time.

The ruled continuity is a balance of perimeter and interior shots. The continuity provides for excellent inside shots that are high percentage and also cause a high number of defensive fouls for your opponents. The offense also provides for offensive rebounding advantages over the defense. Coaches should always attempt to place the best shooters in position to have good shot opportunities and attempt to put the better rebounders in a position advantage to be successful when shots are missed. Try to overload the weakside rebounding area so that you may have a position advantage as well as a numerical advantage over your opposing zone defenders.

Different Entries/Plays Out of the Same Set/Alignment

Different entries/plays can be run out of the same set/alignment to serve as quick-hitters to take advantage of either the offense's strengths, individuals' offensive strengths, the zone's particular weaknesses, or even opposing individual defenders' weaknesses.

Diagrams 2.10 and 2.11 illustrate examples of running two different entries out of the same alignment (the diamond set, Chapter 4) (#2). Diagram 2.10 shows "even," where O1 passes to O3 and exchanges with O2. Meanwhile, O4 has flashed high, looking for an inside gap (#19), and O5 has moved behind the defense before flashing to a side low-post gap (#16).

Diagram 2.11 displays "bam." Instead of flashing to opposite sides of the floor, in bam, both post players (again) duck-in, but return to the post positions on their original sides of the court (#22).

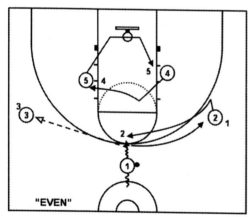

Diagram 2.10

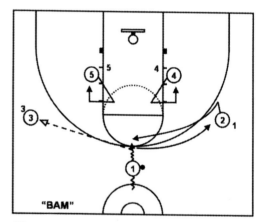

Diagram 2.11

Same Entries/Plays Out of Different Sets/Alignments

The same entry/play or similar entries can be run out of different offensive alignments/sets, which creates what appears to the opposition as a complex zone offense. Actually, it is a multiple (but simple) offense for the offensive team to learn.

The different sets can be implemented to initially distort and attack various zone defenses, still using most of the same basic offensive entries. Diagram 2.12 shows a similar entry out of a different set (the heavy set, Chapter 5) with yet another inside option. In Diagram 2.12, called "heads," O4 will duck-in on O1's dribble, and if he does not receive the pass, he empties out to the new weakside low post spot-up. Meanwhile, O5 begins his move towards the basket, but away from the ball, and cuts back using O4's cut to replace that area on the new ballside low post. O1 passes to a wing, O2, and exchanges with the other wing (Diagram 2.12), which is similar to the other two entries (even and bam).

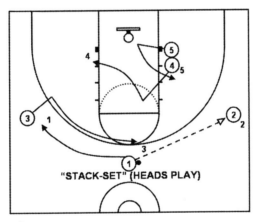

Diagram 2.12

Different Entries/Plays Out of Different Sets/Alignments

Different entries/plays can be run out of the various zone offense sets/alignments. The different sets and the different entries put more pressure on the defense to defend the triple-pronged offensive attack. Weaknesses in the particular zone (or in any of the defensive personnel) can be taken advantage of, while strengths in the initial offensive set (or in the offensive personnel) can be maximized (#3).

Two other entries involving cooperation between the post players and the perimeter players are shown in Diagrams 2.13 and 2.14. In Diagram 2.13, the offense is trying to get a lob pass at the beginning of an offense play called "zoom." A perimeter player (O3 in this case) breaks behind the defense, timing his move to coincide with the two post players (O5 and O4) ducking in the middle of the lane to try to receive a pass in the medium post area. If the post defenders go with the post players, the cutting wing or baseline perimeter player will have a lob pass for a lay-up.

In Diagram 2.13, O3 cuts behind the defense while O4 and O5 use the bam technique described earlier (#16 and #19). At the same time, O1 is using the gap dribble to try to free O2 on the opposite wing area (#12). If no shots develop, the offensive team may have to adjust a player. They would have personnel in the proper spot-ups to then execute the desired continuity offense.

The second entry/play, called "tails," is designed to get a quick lob pass for a score involving only the movement of the two post players. O5 times his move to break behind the defense after O4 has begun the bam move (Diagram 2.14) (#7, #16). O1 makes his gap dribble, looks to bounce pass to O4 on his duck-in cut, and goes on to make a lob pass to O5 or to make wing passes to either O3 or O2.

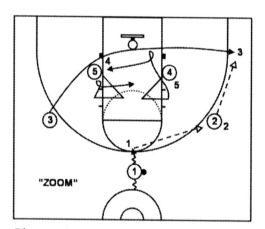

Diagram 2.13

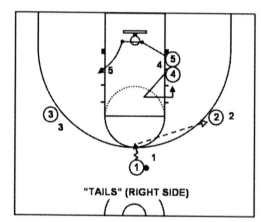

Diagram 2.14

Other Initial Avenues of Attack

Other initial avenues of attack can have a triple-threat to the defense in that the defense must be forced to play the initial alignment, defend the entry, and then defend the designated continuity zone offense. Sideline out-of-bounds (SOB) plays and baseline out-of-bounds (BOB) plays can be much more difficult to defend, especially when they also are three-pronged attacks. All BOB and SOB plays are named with various letters to separate them from all man offense and zone offense entries/plays (Diagrams 2.15 and 2.16 show an example of a BOB play and Diagrams 2.17 and 2.18 of an SOB play).

Each of the out-of-bounds plays should be designed to become quick-scoring, but also to always remain in the zone offense's spot-ups at the conclusion of the play. This approach allows a team to immediately attack the zone defense quickly and smoothly via the zone offense continuity. If the SOB or the BOB play does not produce an immediate score, retaining possession of the ball allows the offensive team to maintain great amounts of pressure on the defenses, as the out-of-bounds play has an immediate transition into an offensive continuity.

Diagrams 2.15 and 2.16 illustrate a baseline out-of-bounds play into the same positions as the baseline zone offense in Chapter 3. No reset of personnel is required. If the out-of-bounds play does not work, the offense goes directly into running the baseline zone offense, described in Chapter 3 (#2 and #5).

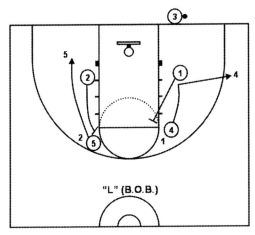

"L" (B.O.B.)

Diagram 2.15

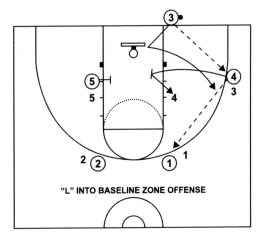

"L" INTO BASELINE ZONE OFFENSE

Diagram 2.16

O3 is the shooter and he takes the ball out-of-bounds. O1 and O2 are the guards and they screen up for O4 and O5, the post men (Diagram 2.15). When O3 passes in bounds to O4 in the corner and O4 passes to O1, O3 steps in bounds and O4 sets a screen for him (Diagram 2.16). If O3 is open for the shot, O1 will pass back to O3. Now take a look at Diagram 3.1, the first one in Chapter 3, describing the baseline zone offense and notice all five offensive players are in the position of Diagram 3.1. Hence, the offense begins the continuity without having to reset.

Diagrams 2.17 and 2.18 displays a side out-of-bounds play into the same basic set position of the baseline zone offense described in Chapter 3. In Diagram 2.15, O3 passes to O2 who has cut around the screen of O1. O4 has made a cut to a gap on the ball side of the court. O3 then breaks around the staggered screens set by O4 and O5 along the baseline. The ball can be reversed from O2 to O1 to O3 for a shot if O3 is open (#10) or O2 can skip pass to O3 (#15).

Again, note that the players end in the same position as Diagram 3.1, which is the first diagram used to explain the baseline offense in Chapter 3. The offense does not have to reset. If no option from the sideline out-of-bounds play (including the post players cutting to openings inside) produces a score, the offense is set and ready to run the baseline zone attack (Chapter 3).

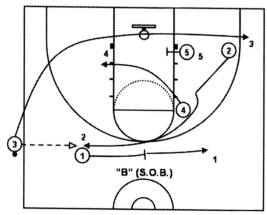

Diagram 2.17

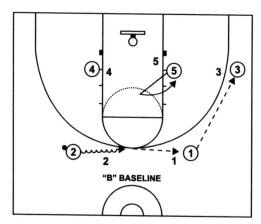

Diagram 2.18

3

The Baseline Zone Continuity Offense, the Pin-Screen Zone Continuity Offense, the 2 Slide Zone Continuity Offense, and the Corners Trap Offense

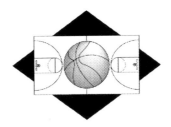

Four distinct and different packages of zone offense continuity spot-ups exist. One group of spot-ups is illustrated with the ball on the right side (Diagram 3.1) with the second diagram showing the ball on the left side (Diagram 3.2). The next four chapters will cover each of these zone offense continuity spot-up packages.

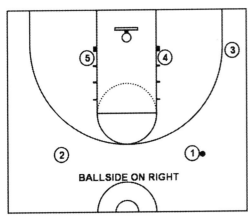

Diagram 3.1

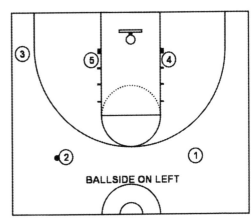

Diagram 3.2

Multiple entries will be presented in each chapter (do not try to teach them all in any one season). When all four chapters are presented, you will have different sets/alignments, different continuities, and a multitude of entries.

Concept #2 uses different sets and entries to be more varied and less predictable to opposing defenses. Chapter 2 was all about Concept #1: Fast break and secondary breaks should complement your zone package. In every newly presented entry, the concepts that correspond with that entry will be noted in parentheses.

Four basic continuities that can be executed from the spot-ups in the chapter are the baseline, the pin-screen, the 2 slide, and the corners trap offense. Each will be presented and discussed. Only entries integrated into the baseline continuity will be presented, but on occasion, those same entries will be shown with one of the other continuities. However, you should easily see that all the entries work with all of the continuities, allowing your players to learn only a few entries, but the offense will still look multiple.

The baseline continuity has multiple options, which can greatly help prevent the offense from being predictable and scout-able by opposing defensive teams (#2). This offense has the capability to incorporate offensive players' individual strengths and stay within the structure of the zone offense (#5). The baseline zone offense attacks the zone defense's weaknesses (#3). The baseline zone offense (with the even front) is most effective against odd front zone defenses such as a 1-2-2 or a 1-3-1 zone (#4).

Your team can easily use one or more of the secondary fast breaks because they all lead into spot-up positions of the baseline zone offense (#1). This maneuver allows the offense to continue its attack on the defense without any interruptions or pauses to regroup and reorganize, if the secondary break does not produce a quick score.

The five spot-up positions allow for maximum offensive rebounding effectiveness for the offensive team (#8). Each offensive player has distinct and clearly understood offensive rebounding responsibilities that should be executed by every player (#9). The baseline zone offense also has specific clear-cut defensive transition responsibilities (#7).

Placement of Personnel

The standard numbering system will be used to explain this zone offense:

- O1 should be the point guard
- O2 should be the big guard
- O3 is the small forward
- O4 is the power forward
- O5 is the center

Players O2 and O3 should be very similar in their overall offensive skills and abilities, in that their two assignments in this offense can be interchangeable. The zone offense will be more effective if the perimeter players (O1, O2, and O3) are good perimeter shooters that can get their shots off quickly off the pass. They should know how to effectively use the different types of zone dribbles and passes used to vertically and horizontally stretch the defense (#10, #21).

The best defender of the two perimeter players out on top of the offense is assigned the sole responsibility of getting back on defense and is called the tailback. The other smaller perimeter player's responsibility entails both rebounding and also getting back on defense. That player is half rebounder and half defensive safety and is appropriately called the halfback (#8, #9).

The designated post players (O4 and O5) must know how and when to make the appropriate cuts on the interior of the zone (#22). The two post players (O4 and O5) must be able to catch the various types of passes made to them so they can effectively score inside with a variety of post moves (#25).

Spot-up Locations and Descriptions

The baseline zone offense is a specialized personnel zone offense where each player-position has a name that specifically describes the main location of that player-position (#5). Diagrams 3.1 and 3.2 show the five spot-up positions on both the left and the right sides of the court.

The ballside wing is always on the ballside wing area, which is just outside the three-point line and approximately halfway between the free throw lane line vertically extended with the free throw line extended (in an area called the elbow area) and the sideline. He can be either O1 or O2, whoever is the better interior passer and gap dribbler. The weakside wing is in the same location out on top of the zone as the ballside wing, but he is always on the offensive weakside of the court. He can either be O2 or O1, although he ideally is the better perimeter shooter (off of the pass) of the two players.

The ballside corner is always lined up in the ballside deep corner, just outside of the three-point line. Within one or two passes after the ball has been reversed from the deep-corner to the other side, the ballside corner will switch to the new ballside of the court. He is called the ballside corner because he always makes cuts along the baseline to switch from one ballside deep corner to the new ballside deep corner. The ballside corner most likely will be O3, but could ideally be interchanged with O2. O2 and O3 could most likely be very similar in ability levels and have the same skills needed to be successful.

The ballside post is the post player that starts on the ballside. At times, he starts as a high-post player or at the ballside elbow post area and slides down to the medium low-post area when the ball is passed or dribbled down to the deep corner. This post player should position himself by straddling the first notch above the block and never be allowed to be pushed below the first notch, otherwise he would have terrible angles to attack the basket effectively. The weakside post also ends up on the first notch above the block, but always on the weakside of the offense.

The two post players are always O4 and O5 and the location of the basketball dictates which one is called the ballside post and which is called the weakside post. When the ball is reversed to the opposite side of the floor, the original ballside post player becomes the new weakside post and the original weakside post becomes the new ballside post. These two post players are identical, except both start (and remain) on one particular side of the lane.

Options Off Original Set/Alignment

All of the options shown and discussed, while shown only on the right side, can and must be executed on both sides of the court. Each of these options is interchangeable and can be used on any of the various zone offense continuities, whether the coaching staff elects to use the baseline continuity, the pin-screen continuity, the 2 slide continuity, or the corners continuity. These options will be presented first from the spot-ups on the right. Then the continuities will be offered. Finally, movement into those continuities will be presented.

Diagram 3.3 displays the spot-up positions. These are the areas of the court where the players will work on their shots during the shooting drills.

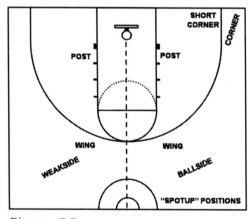

Diagram 3.3

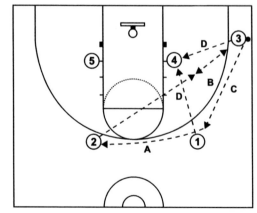

Diagram 3.4

Diagram 3.4 exhibits the original triangle principle of attacking zone defenses. O1 has the option of passing to the corner to O3 (#5), or passing inside to O4 (#21, #22, #23, #24, #25). Once O3 has the ball, he can pass inside to O4 if he does not have an open shot (#13). Remember, any pass inside compels the perimeter players to reposition themselves for a pass back outside (#21).

The pass from O1 to O2 is a reverse pass (#10). This pass activates the baseline continuity, unless O3 remains in his deep-corner position, which occurs in Diagram 3.4. Now O2 can skip pass to O3 and all the options are still available (#15). O3 also has the skip pass back to O2 as an option.

Post players, O4 and O5, can make use of cuts to the open gaps while the perimeter is in the stationary mode of the offense (#22). Diagram 3.5 exhibits the duck in cut. These cuts now are part of some of the entries (before the continuity begins), or the post men can run these cuts as the continuity is being executed.

Diagram 3.6 displays the gap cut by O5 (#22). This option is especially powerful when O1 has the ball (from Diagram 3.4), making the freeze dribble towards O2 on the weakside, and O1, O3, and O4 are executing the triangle overload (#12).

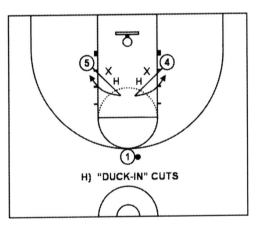

H) "DUCK-IN" CUTS

Diagram 3.5

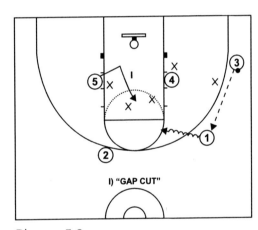

I) "GAP CUT"

Diagram 3.6

If the primary break did not score, if the secondary break did not score, and if the stationary ball movement of the basic set did not score, movement is required (#1, #5). Patience is a virtue in attacking a zone (#26). The following explains some minor movements before going into the continuity.

Diagram 3.7 shows a pull dribble and replace technique discussed in Chapter 1. O3 dribbles away from the corner, taking his defender with him, possibly even freezing the defender near O2 (#12, #16). Meanwhile, O5 has cut to the short corner for a throw back pass from O3. O4 has tried to find the gap in the middle of the zone (#22).

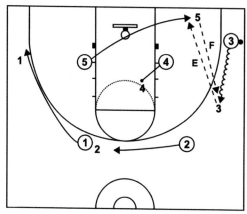
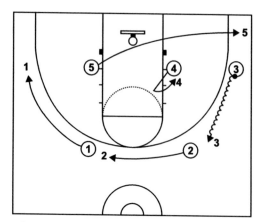

Diagram 3.7   Diagram 3.8

If O3's defender followed him, then one defender must cover both O4 and O5. This opening in the defense should result in an easy score (#3). You will notice that O2 has taken the original position of O1 and O1 has cut to the corner behind the zone (#16). The offense is now in the same basic alignment, just to the left side of the court (Diagram 3.7). The stationary options discussed earlier are now available on the other side of the court (#26).

Diagram 3.8 demonstrates a replacement cut by the weakside post player to the deep corner. O5 replaces O3 as he dribbles from the corner, and O2 replaces O1, as O1 replaces O5 in the weakside (#12, #16, #22). Remember any pass inside compels the perimeter to find the gaps on the perimeter (#21).

Diagram 3.9 illustrates O2 drifting to the corner and O1 making a skip pass to O2 (#15). O1 fills the spot vacated by O2 and O3 fills O1's vacated spot. The offense is

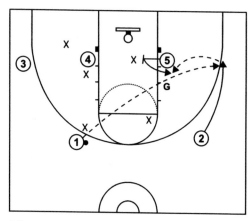
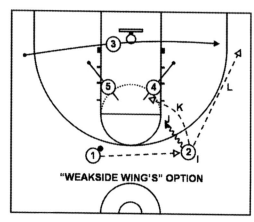

Diagram 3.9   Diagram 3.10

still in their stationary positions with all the previous discussed options available. O5 sets the pin-screen for O2 to utilize before posting up on the new ballside low post (#18).

Now, the following involves some movement by showing the continuities. Diagram 3.10 exhibits the baseline zone continuity. O3, who can begin in any corner, runs the baseline behind the defensive backline, looking for the post players to pin-screen or duck into the middle of the zone (#16, #18, #22). This play is identical to the baseline out-of-bounds play presented in Chapter 2.

The Baseline Zone Offense's Continuity Rules

In the baseline zone continuity (Diagram 3.10), when the ballside wing, O2, has the ball, he has the following nine options:

- Shoot off of the pass, or penetrate and shoot off of the dribble (#13).
- Pass inside to the ballside post (#23).
- Down-pass to the ballside corner (#17).
- Freeze dribble across the center line to attack the next defender over (#9, #12).
- Look to hit either the weakside post or the ballside post who are both ducking in to the dotted circle (#23, #24, #25).
- Pass to the weakside wing (#9).
- Quickly throw the ball back to the ballside corner (before he has run his baseline cut to the other side of the floor) (#17).
- Throw a lob pass toward the basket for the ballside corner as he makes his cut along the baseline (#23).
- Throw a skip pass to O3 if he is in the weakside corner (#15).

When the weakside wing, O1, receives the ball, he has the following options:
- Shoot quickly off of the pass (#13).
- Drive and shoot, or use the dribbles (freeze, gap, or pull) (#11, #12, #13).
- Make an inside pass to the original weakside post or the original ballside post that are both ducking in (#23).
- Make a down-pass to the ballside corner who is cutting to the new ballside deep corner (#17).

When the ballside corner, O3, has the ball in the deep corner, he can look to:
- Shoot off of the pass (#13).
- Drive and then shoot, using the dribbles (freeze, gap, or pull) (#12, #13).

- Skip pass diagonally across the floor to the weakside wing (O1) (#15).
- Up-pass to the ballside wing (O1).

Now, coaches can combine some of these individual maneuvers within the baseline continuity. Diagram 3.11 illustrates the freeze dribble being run within the frameworks of the baseline continuity against a 2-3 zone (#9, #12). O1 uses the freeze dribble to compel A to help B on defense (#12). O2 has executed his flare cut. O3 has run the baseline in the continuity. O4 and O5 both have made gap cuts (#16, #22). Defender D must cover O2, O5, and O3, which, of course, is impossible (Diagram 3.11) (#3, #4, #5).

Diagram 3.11 shows the problems the defense faces. Should D get outside and cover O2, then C must decide between covering O5 or O3, another impossibility. If the offense is patient, it will overload the coverage of even the best defenses (#26).

If the offense does not take advantage and get the good shot, it is because they did not see it. However, even in that case, the baseline continuity is set for all the options to begin again. All five players are back in the baseline continuity offense's spot-up locations (Diagram 3.12) (#26).

Now, the baseline continuity can easily become one of the other continuities, giving the offense a multiple look. Diagrams 3.13 and 3.14 will be used to show these conversions from the baseline continuity into the triple post zone offense discussed in Chapter 6. A simple inside gap cut by O5 gets you into the triple post offense (Diagram 3.13) (#2, #22). Now all the options available to the baseline continuity are available to the triple post continuity and vice versa. To then get back into the baseline continuity, O4 empties out to the opposite post while O5 slides down and replaces the cutting O4 (#22). In Diagram 3.14, the three perimeter players remain in the same spot-up locations.

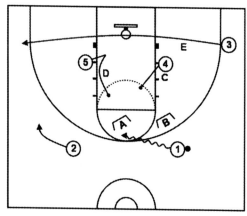

Diagram 3.11

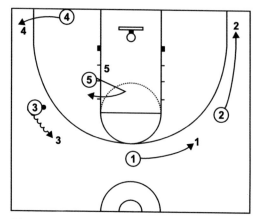

Diagram 3.12

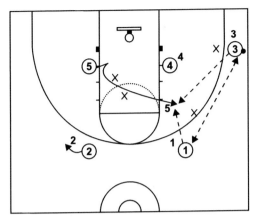

Diagram 3.13

Diagram 3.14

Loop Option

Diagrams 3.15 through 3.18 will show the loop option of the baseline continuity. While showing the loop option, the offense will move from the baseline continuity into the heavy or rotation continuity discussed in Chapter 5. From these examples, you will be able to see how the three work together to form a multiple offense: same entries, different sets; different entries, different sets; and different entries, same sets.

In Diagram 3.15, O1 tried to use the freeze dribble to free O2, O3, or O5 in the baseline continuity (#12). It failed either because of poor execution or great defense. However, the offense does not stop (#5, #26).

O2 cuts to the opposite side of the court after passing to O3 (Diagram 3.16) (#7). O1 sets a screen on defender B for a possible skip pass from O3 to O2 for the weakside shot (#15). O1 and O2 basically exchange the wing area spot-up locations.

Diagram 3.17 shows the offense continuing into the pull dribble and replace technique (#12, #19). O3 dribbles out of the corner and O4 replaces him on the perimeter. C, the inside defender, must decide to cover O5 or O4 because D must follow O3 until A picks O3 up out on the wing.

The offense is now in the 1-3-1 spot-ups of the heavy or rotation (Chapter 5) continuity (Diagram 3.17) (#2, #5). The offense can now run the options discussed in Chapter 5; or, the offense can let O2 drift to the baseline while O1 floats to the weakside wing and O4 steps out to the deep-corner. The offense would then be in the alignment of the baseline continuity (as well as the pin-screen, the 2 slide, and the corners continuities) (Diagram 3.18).

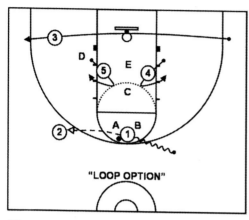

"LOOP OPTION"

Diagram 3.15

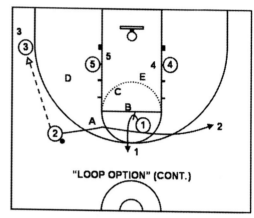

"LOOP OPTION" (CONT.)

Diagram 3.16

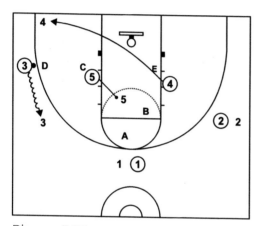

Diagram 3.17

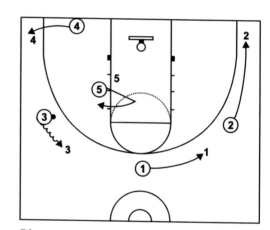

Diagram 3.18

A skip pass from O3 to O2, and O2 using the pull dribble to the corner is shown in Diagram 3.19 (#12, #15). O5 screens for O4 for a possible lob pass to O5 from O2 after O5 seals off the defender he screened (#18). If none of these options is open for a score, the offense is in the baseline continuity (#26). O2 could also look to hit O4 posting-up on the new ballside low post.

Diagram 3.20 illustrates a pull dribble followed by a replacement cut by O4, which is the basic cut of the pin screen continuity (#19). As O3 pull dribbles, O4 replaces him. A throwback pass from O3 to O4 in the short corner might distort the defense for an open shot (#4, #7, #19). O4 should immediately look inside to O5 (#20), or look to skip pass to O2 (#15). A pass inside to O5, who has cut to a gap (#22), should impel O5 to look for a pass to O4 in short corner or cutting along the baseline (#20) or to skip pass to O2 (#15). The offense has moved from the baseline continuity to the heavy continuity in this one option.

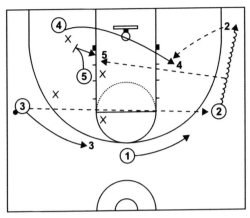

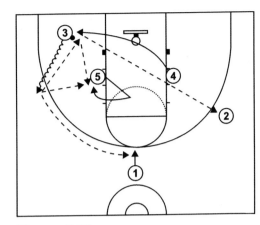

Diagram 3.19   Diagram 3.20

Diagram 3.21 is a continuation of Diagram 3.20. O3 was unable to pass inside to either O4 or O5 or skip pass to O2. Instead, O3 pull dribbles or even uses a freeze or gap dribble once he is at the wing, until O3 reverses the ball to O1 and on to O2. O2 dribbles into the corner while O5 sets a screen for a possible pass to O4 or a lob pass to O5 after he seals off the defender he initially back screened for O4. The team is now in the basic baseline continuity offense's spot-ups locations.

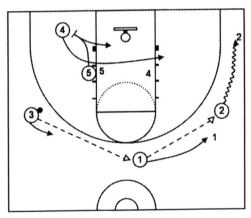

Diagram 3.21

Offensive Rebounding and
Transition Responsibilities

The baseline zone offense should have the three potentially best offensive rebounders assigned the name of fullback, with their main assignment and responsibility of crashing the offensive boards hard. The remaining two players have other transition and rebounding responsibilities (#8). The three fullbacks should form a triangular cup around the basket, two to three feet away. If the rebound cannot be secured with two hands by one of the fullbacks, he sometimes might have to back tip the ball out to the halfback. Upon seeing that the opponents have secured the defensive rebound, the two biggest fullbacks should then run the lanes as if they were on an offensive fast break. Sprinting quickly in their offensive lanes while getting back on defense not only gets them back on defense, but also may cause them to literally run into some of the opposition's outlet passes (#9).

The fourth best rebounder is the half-rebounder and half-defensive safety and is called the halfback. His responsibility is two-fold, divided equally between offensive rebounding and getting back on the defensive transition. The halfback should quickly go to the elbow area on the side of the court opposite to where the shot was taken—the weakside elbow area. When he sees the defensive rebound is secured, he should get out and run his assigned offensive fast break lane and sprint to the other end of the floor as quickly as possible. The halfback might also run into an interception or at least slow down the opposition's fast break (#8, #9).

The zone offense's smallest defender has only one major responsibility and it is solely to get back on defense to prevent the opponent from getting easy scores from their fast breaks. He is called the tailback because his only responsibility is to get his tail back on defense. When the shot is taken, he is to sprint back (from wherever he was when the shot was actually taken) to the edge of the center jump-circle, with absolutely no offensive rebounding responsibilities to hold him back. Upon seeing that the opposition has full control of the ball, the tailback should then quickly sprint to the opposite free throw line to force the opposition's fast break into making as many passes as it has to (to force the opposition to take as much time as possible). Doing so allows the original offensive team more time for the halfback and three fullbacks to get back to also help protect their basket (Diagram 3.22).

When the shot is taken and missed, the three fullbacks and the halfback should all rush the weakside of the zone with offensive rebounders, to outnumber and overload the area where the majority of the missed shots will fall. If an offensive rebound is not grabbed, they should immediately be prepared to run the defensive fast break.

The three fullbacks and the one halfback should remember the following concepts when offensively rebounding missed shots from the zone offense:

- The majority of missed shots fall on the opposite side of the court from where they were taken.

- The longer the shot, the longer the rebound from most missed shots—so they should not get drawn too close to the basket.

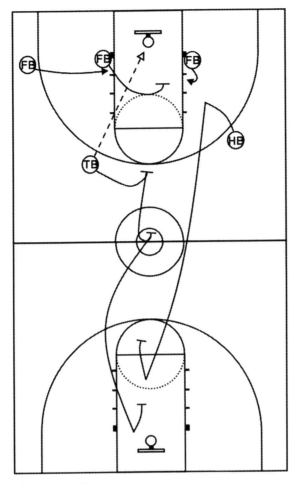

Diagram 3.22

- Players in zone offenses have distinct advantages in gaining rebounding advantages over zone defenders, so they need to take advantage of that fact and be aggressive on the boards.

Every one of the five players must meet their responsibilities and carry out their assignments in the offensive rebounding and the defensive transition segment of the zone offense for the baseline zone offense to be as efficient as it can possibly be (#8, #9).

Alignments/Sets into the Zone Continuity Offense

The alignments and sets for the baseline zone offense are as important as the entries are to the whole zone offensive package. Regardless of the alignments and regardless of the entries that are run, all must end in the zone offense continuity spot-ups, so that the continuity offense can be continued with no pause or letup. Attacking the zone defense's weaknesses or taking advantage of specific offensive players' individual strengths can only be accomplished if the offense is set up initially in particular zone offense sets (#3, #4, #5).

For obvious reasons, the larger number of sets and entries that a zone offense possesses, the harder it is for opponents to scout, prepare for, and ultimately defend (#2). If a team can mentally handle multiple sets, it is wise to expand the zone offense package. The multiple sets could be used to show the defense different looks, while keeping the same plays that lead into the same continuity zone offense.

Entries/Plays into the Zone Offense Continuity

Entries are simply quick-hitters that attempt to score after specific offensive action and within one or two passes. Each of the entries is designed to make sure that all five offensive players will end up in specific spot-up positions if the entry fails in its attempt to score. If all five players end up in the correct spot-up positions and a shot is taken, the offensive rebounding action should be at its maximum effectiveness (#8, #9). Entries from the baseline zone offense can easily move into the zone offense continuity from the spot-up positions, putting even more pressure on the opposition's defense. Each zone offensive alignment can offer as many different entries as the coaching staff and the players can successfully utilize. The more varied that a team can be with its entries, the less predictable and less scoutable that team is (#2).

Other Continuities with the
Same Zone Offense Spot-Up Positions

Four continuities with these spot-ups are the baseline, the pin-screen, the 2 slide, and the corners. The baseline continuity was already shown and the other three follow. It is important you note that any entry that has been discussed so far will work from any of the continuities.

Diagram 3.23 shows the pin screen continuity. The players begin in a position where they will be at the end of the secondary break or at the end of half-court entries with O3 having the ball (Diagram 3.23). As the ball is reversed from O3 to O1 to O2, O4 cuts off O5's screen and O3 fills the space vacated by O4 (#17, #19). O1 and O2 should exchange places after O2's down-pass to O3.

To continue the continuity, O1 would pass the ball back to O2 on the new weakside. While this pass was occurring, O5 would break off O3's pin screen and O4 would replace O5. The ball is moved back and forth between O1 and O2 while the three inside players (O3, O4, and O5) continue pin screens, cut off the pin screens, and the make replacement cuts.

All the options discussed earlier work with this continuity also. For example, the freeze dribble by either of the guards still has the other guard open and a cutter along the baseline (#2, #3, #4, #5, #17).

The freeze dribble entry (Diagram 3.24) involves O1 dribble driving toward O2's defender, hoping to freeze him (#12). Meanwhile, O3 has screened for O5 to run the pin screen continuity (#18). O4 replaces O5 (#19). O3 cuts to a gap after setting the pin screen for O5 (#22). O1 now can pass to O3 (Pass Z), O2 (Pass Y), O4 (Pass V), or skip pass to O5 (Pass W) (#15).

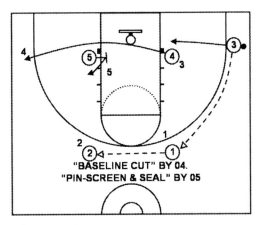

Diagram 3.23   Diagram 3.24

An effective option in the pin screen continuity is the throwback counter option (Diagram 3.25). O4 cuts to a space above O5 and they set a double screen for O3. O5 pin screens and then cuts to the opposite block, replacing O3. This action can continue as a double screen along the baseline with the normal pin screen continuity, or to execute a second throwback counter option (#15).

When your personnel permits an outside/inside exchange of offensive players, Diagram 3.26 shows a method of doing so. O5 starts the pin screen continuity by pin screening for O4. Instead of O2 replacing O4, O2 breaks outside to replace O1 who began the continuity by running the freeze dribble entry. After O3 passes to O4, O3 fills the vacant original spot of O4. O1 replaces O3. This move repositions O4 in the new ballside corner spot-up position, O5 on the new ballside low post, O3 on the weakside low post, O1 on the ballside wing, and O2 back at the weakside wing. The pin screen continuity offense has all the spot-up locations correctly filled with the proper offensive personnel filling their spot-ups (#26).

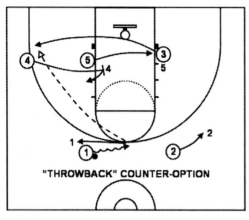

"THROWBACK" COUNTER-OPTION

Diagram 3.25

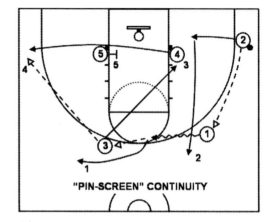

"PIN-SCREEN" CONTINUITY

Diagram 3.26

The post men can still operate the entries/plays (bam, head, and zoom) discussed in Chapter 1. This maneuver makes the entire offense look multiple, but it is really just the same entries with different possible continuities (#6).

The next continuity that is discussed with the same spot-up locations is the 2 slide continuity (Diagram 3.27). After no score developed from the designated entry, all personnel are again at the proper spot-up locations necessary for the designated continuity offense to immediately begin. When O1 receives the up-pass from O3, he freeze dribbles towards the perimeter defender closest to O2 (#12). O4 empties out of the original ballside block, disappearing behind the defense (#16), while O5 makes a gap cut anywhere into the lane, looking for the ball (#22). If O5 does not receive the pass from O1, he ends up on the block on the opposite side of the lane. O4 also ends up on the block opposite of where he started. O3 runs along the baseline from the original ballside corner to the opposite deep-corner area (#19). O1 looks to hit O5 on the diagonal gap cut while O4 is hiding out behind the defense's backline. If O3 does not have an open shot or an inside pass to O4, O3 then throws a skip pass to O2 on a freeze dribble and pitch pass (#9, #12, #13, #17).

While the spot-up locations are almost identical, the corner offense has a completely different identity and purpose. This offense is used to attack opposing teams' half-court pressure defense, not passive zone defense. Therefore, no entries/ plays initiate the offense before flowing into the continuity offenses. All four perimeter locations are one to five feet further out to spread the defense. This offense can be used as a semi-delay, a delay game, or a half-court trap offense.

When the ball is passed down in the deep corner (O1 to O3), the weakside baseline player (O5 in this case) dives to the currently vacant weakside low post spot-up position. The current ballside low-post player (O4) chases the ball from one low post location to the high post elbow, and then to the opposite side of the lane to the elbow area, down to that side's low post area when the ball is reversed. The current ballside corner player (O5 or O3) always steps out to the deep corner, while the weakside corner (O3 or O5) dives to the weakside block.

You can quickly change from one of these continuities to another by simply calling out the continuity you want to run. They are all interchangeable; therefore, you have a complex, multiple zone offense that is not too difficult for your players.

In later chapters, moving from one continuity offense to the next, with minimal movement of personnel, will be shown. In the last section of this chapter, ideas on movement breakdown drills will be given, while Chapter 7 will present some shooting breakdown drills.

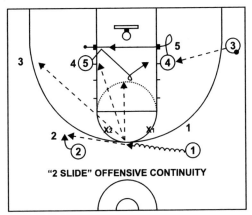

"2 SLIDE" OFFENSIVE CONTINUITY

Diagram 3.27

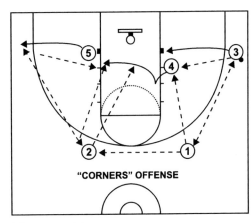

"CORNERS" OFFENSE

Diagram 3.28

Breakdown Drills for the Zone Offense

A good coaching staff can form their own drills to strengthen individual players' offensive fundamentals that are needed to make the offense more effective. Shooting drills, passing and catching drills, screening and cutting drills, offensive rebounding drills, and defensive transition drills are some of the types of drills that should be created to improve the overall effectiveness of the zone offense.

When these fundamentals are drilled while running the movements of the offense, two results occur. First, the offense is being taught and re-taught each day that the drills are run. Second, the spot-ups are also being taught and re-taught. To make drills out of movement is to run only one part of the offense at a time. These breakdowns will be shown for the 2-3 sets (Chapter 3). Coaches can create the same types of drills for the other sets in the next three chapters.

Shooting drills for particular players can be created at certain locations, where players are most likely going to shoot the ball during the execution of the offense. Most of the shooting drills are set up in the 55-second offensive/shooting drill format, where three players are involved in each drill (Chapter 7). One player in the 55-second offensive/shooting drills is called the rebounder, one is called the passer, and one called the shooter. Using this type of drill, the coaching staff can place the passer and the shooter in the same positions where they would be located in the actual zone offense you are utilizing. The rebounder basically chases down all shots (made or missed that the shooter takes) and then outlet-passes them to the passer, using the proper rebounding and passing techniques. The passer then delivers the ball to the shooter, using his proper passing techniques. Shots are practiced and passes are practiced only in the locations that players would normally take them in games and in the context of the zone offense. After the 55-seconds expire, the shooter becomes the new rebounder, the rebounder rotates to become the next passer, and the passer becomes the new shooter. After another 55-second period expires, all three players rotate again. After the third 55-second time period is concluded, the players can start the drill again, but on the opposite side of the court. Within six minutes, all three players in each group of players have experienced two separate minutes of rebounding and making outlet passes, two minutes of working on passing skills, and two minutes of shooting from the same spots where they take their shots in the offense.

One of the best ways to make the shooting drills as game-realistic as it can be is to apply some type of pressure on each player performing the drill. One method is to place some form of performance competition either between individuals, or teams of individuals (to promote teamwork), or all groups going against a common opponent. Another way to make the drills more game-realistic is to make sure that each offensive fundamental drill has winners and losers, with the losers having some form of a minor consequence.

Diagram 3.29 illustrates a drill for the baseline cutter, usually O3, and the post player, O4 or O5. A post player can be the rebounder, R, and make an outlet pass to the cutter, P (#1). So you are working on the outlet pass of your fast break. P can shoot or pass inside to the post player, S (#22, #24, #25). After passing to S, P should relocate around the perimeter for a possible pass back out from the post (#21). This drill permits the baseline cutter and the post to work together on the baseline continuity, the pin screen continuity, the 2 slide continuity, and the corner continuity.

The following drill allows the guards and the post players to work out of the spot-ups of the zone offense continuities just discussed (Diagram 3.30). P, on both sides of the court, is working on his freeze, pull, or gap dribble (#12), while the post men are working on their cuts to the open gaps, their body positioning, and their past moves (#20, #22, #23, #24, #25). On the pass to the post, P should reposition himself for the possible kickout pass (#21). Again, a rebounder, R, can be used to throw an outlet

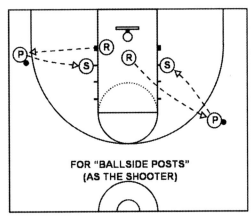

FOR "BALLSIDE POSTS"
(AS THE SHOOTER)

Diagram 3.29

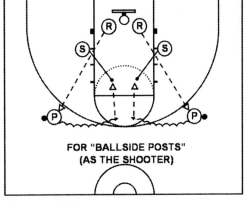

FOR "BALLSIDE POSTS"
(AS THE SHOOTER)

Diagram 3.30

pass, allowing the players to work on their fast break off of missed shots (#1). Either of the players (P or S) may shoot; and on the shots, the players should go to their transition positions (either rebounding or defensive) (#8, #9).

Diagram 3.31 displays the cooperative effort between the guard and the baseline cutter. S cuts to the corner for a pass from P. P can make this pass from a stationary position, or P can use one of the three dribble techniques before passing to S (#12). When S catches the ball, he should be ready to shoot, drive, or pass back out to P (#13, #14). Again, a rebounder, R, can be used to work on the outlet pass (#1), if you feel the need to work on this phase of the fast break. Otherwise, when the shot is taken, both players go to their transition positions (#8, #9).

For a three-perimeter player drill (the two guards and the baseline cutter), using Diagram 3.31, the players would work on only one side of the floor. This positioning

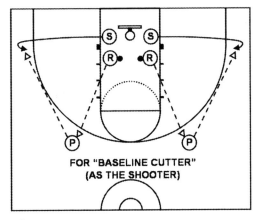

FOR "BASELINE CUTTER"
(AS THE SHOOTER)

Diagram 3.31

opens up the skip pass from P to S on the other side of the floor (#15). You could also work on the three dribbles by allowing the guards to execute the freeze dribble, for example. If the right guard executed the freeze dribble, then the left guard would cut away from the dribble a few feet. The pass can then be made between the two players before passing to the corner. The three players are learning the offense, executing the fundamentals, and going into transition mode on any shot.

Diagram 3.32 brings in a fourth player: the three perimeter players and a post player. O1 executes the freeze dribble (#12). O4 sets the screen for the cutting O3 (#18). O4 then cuts to the open gap (#20, #22, #23, #24, #25). Everything about these spot-ups now comes into play: the skip passes (#15), the dribble moves (#12), the corner cuts (#2, #3, #4, #5), the post moves (#20, #22, #23, #24, #25), as well as the repositioning when a pass goes inside (#21). The baseline cutter, O3, could even use the pull dribble, by dribbling out to the wing area, and O4 steps out in the perimeter and replaces the dribbler (O3) (#19). The players are learning the offense as well as drilling on the fundamentals. When a shot is taken, the four go into transition mode (#8, #9). All players should be ready to shoot, pass, or dribble when they receive the pass (#13, #14).

Skip passes from the corner are also available to the opposite guard (#15). Skip passes are such an integral part of all the offensive sets that you might want to drill on it in a two man setting. Diagram 3.33 shows such structure. The P's and the S's can skip pass several times before shooting. You can include a rebounder if you need to work on the outlet pass (#1). The skip pass can originate from the deep corner to the new weakside wing area, or the ball can be outletted to the wing and then skip passed to the new weakside deep corner to be shot.

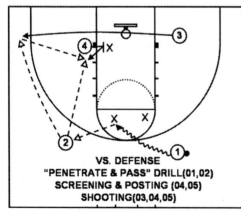

VS. DEFENSE
"PENETRATE & PASS" DRILL(O1,O2)
SCREENING & POSTING (O4,O5)
SHOOTING(O3,O4,O5)

Diagram 3.32

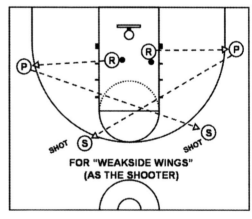

FOR "WEAKSIDE WINGS"
(AS THE SHOOTER)

Diagram 3.33

Conclusion

The baseline zone offense is an offense that utilizes many sound zone offensive concepts and philosophies that will take advantage of many of the defense's weaknesses. Individual player assignments and responsibilities in every phase of the game are clearly distributed to particular players to make the offense a carefully planned out zone offense—one that is efficient and productive both offensively in terms of rebounding, as well as in transition defense.

Since the baseline zone continuity offense can use various entries out of different initial sets, this multiplicity advantage allows the offense to attack different types of zone defenses that have even or odd fronts. Offensively, once the ball is in the deep corner, most zone defenses have deployed their personnel in about the same manner, regardless of its initial alignment (they are in a 2-3 zone and you know they slide out of that into their basic zone). Therefore, the continuity's attack is similar against every zone defense (once the ball is on the baseline).

You can exercise as much control as you wish. You can call from the bench the entry/play you wish at any time, as well as the particular continuity desired. You can have your post players executing gap cuts while your perimeter can use freeze, pull, or gap dribbles during the execution of the continuity offense.

Even though all three zone offenses have the capabilities of having multiple options that can be incorporated within them, the offenses remain simple offenses for players to learn and also be able to perform. With each position being a specialized position, each player clearly knows his responsibilities and assignments. Each position player can hone his offensive skills and be able to perform them at a high degree of efficiency and productivity. Developing and utilizing breakdown drills for each position allows players to become effective at that position as well as being able to continually learn and understand that particular position's responsibilities and assignments. As each individual player improves in his knowledge and understanding of the offense and improves individual offensive skills, the offensive team improves in the various continuity offenses.

The offensive philosophy is such that it should be required that the primary fast break and any full court press offenses that are implemented should have a smooth, easy, and immediate transition into the secondary fast break. The secondary fast break must then have the capabilities and the compatibilities of flowing immediately into one of the zone offenses, making every one of the fast break opportunities a vehicle to not only attempt to score, but to also get into the specific continuity zone offense. This approach prevents the opposition's zone defense from being able to reorganize and set up their zone defense properly. With one or more of their players possibly out of position, their defense could tremendously weaken. Following this approach gives the offense still another advantage over the defense.

4

The Diamond Zone Continuity Offense

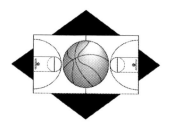

Introduction to the Zone Offense

For the diamond zone offense to be successfully run, the continuity zone offense requires that every offensive player start in the proper offensive positions or locations (called spot-ups), and follow the specific rules for each type of pass that can be made. This offense not only attacks the zone defense's weaknesses (#3), but has the flexibility and the adaptability to be able to integrate offensive players' individual strengths within the actual structure of the zone offense (#5). This offense also has multiple options to help prevent the offense from being predictable and scoutable by opposing teams (#2).

Moreover, these spot-ups can quickly convert into different spot-ups, making the entries of both this chapter and Chapter 3 interchangeable (#2). And from Diagram 1.3, Chapter 1, you can easily see how the secondary break evolves into the spot-up locations of the diamond zone continuity offense (#1).

Placement of Personnel

As in all zone offenses, the better the perimeter players are in their perimeter shooting abilities, the more effective the zone offense is. The diamond zone offense stretches the defense both vertically and horizontally, besides being able to probe the inside of the zone defense. It is very important that all three of the perimeter players know and are able to use the various types of zone dribbles and passes that should be utilized (#11, #12, #13, #14). The two post players and the best rebounder of the three perimeter players are assigned as full-time offensive rebounders (#9). The best defender of the two remaining perimeter players is assigned the sole responsibility of getting back on defense, while the remaining perimeter player is assigned a responsibility that entails both rebounding and also getting back on defense (#8).

The two post players (most likely O4 and O5) are the full-time rebounders and they must be able to catch the various types of passes made to them and also be able to effectively score inside with various offensive post moves (#20, #21, #22, #23). Post players must be able to read the defense, particularly the interior defense, and attack it accordingly. These two players must be able to work well together and be able to read each other's interior cuts (#20).

Spot-up Locations and Descriptions

The diamond zone offense's five proper spot-up locations are illustrated in Diagram 4.1. After any of the entries take place (without a score or a turnover), the ball will result at one of the wing positions. That position is called the ballside wing, with the four other locations being the offside wing, the ballside post, the weakside post, and the point location. With the ball being at one wing position and the other four positions being filled, the rules of the continuity of the diamond zone offense can then be properly executed.

On all reverse passes from the ballside wing area to the point area, the current weakside low-post player reads the cut of the current ballside post. The ballside post reads the post defender and always breaks away from that specific defender (Diagram 4.2). If the ballside post makes the high cut, the weakside post makes the low cut.

Diagram 4.1

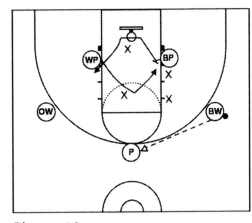

Diagram 4.2

Diagram 4.2 illustrates the ballside low-post making the low cut and the weakside low-post the high cut—a duck-in cut. After the cuts are made, both post players cross the lane and end up posting up on the opposite sides of the lane.

Special Terminology

The basic spot-up positions are defined with the location of the ball dictating that side of the court as being the ballside, and the opposite side called the weakside or the offside.

The point spot-up position, just outside of the three-point line, is centered at the top of the key, while the ballside wing and the weakside wing spot-up positions are just outside of the three-point line at the free-throw line extended. The ballside post and the weakside post spot-up positions are located on the first notch above the block. When occasionally needed, the ballside short-corner and the weakside short-corner positions are located directly on the baseline midway between the free-throw lane line and the sideline, on their respective sides of the court (Diagram 4.3) (#4, #17).

Diagram 4.4 shows the basic diamond continuity. O1 passes to O3, which is the signal for a perimeter exchange between O1 and O2 and a post exchange by O4 and O5 (#19). The cuts do not have to be as simple as shown in Diagram 4.4. Many other options could possibly be executed. The various entries are the subject of the remainder of this chapter.

Cuts from the post area to the dotted circle in the middle of the free-throw lane are called duck-ins (Diagram 4.5). Diagram 4.5 is the first option discussed. O1 is using the gap dribble, trying to free O3 or O2 of their defender by forcing the two front defenders of a 2-1-2 zone to both cover the dribbler (#12). Meanwhile, O4 and O5 execute the duck-ins/cuts (#22).

Diagram 4.6 exhibits O4 making a flash pivot cut (also called a gap cut) from behind the defense. O5 has the option of rolling to the other side or stepping out to the short corner or the deep corner. When O2 passed to O3, O2 and O1 execute the perimeter exchange part of the basic continuity after the wing pass from O1 to O3 is made (#3, #4, #6, #22).

Post players are not limited to any one specific route or cut. They have the freedom to find an opening or any holes in the middle of the zone defense and attack that specific weakness, also attacking the defense from behind (#3, #4, #16, #22).

Diagram 4.7 illustrates another choice of options using only post moves and a perimeter exchange. O5 cuts to the corner or short corner from behind the backline of the zone, while O4 executes a duck-in or a gap cut as the wing pass is made (#3, #4, #16, #22).

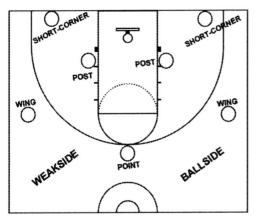

Diagram 4.3

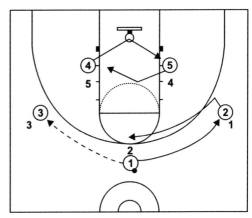

Diagram 4.4

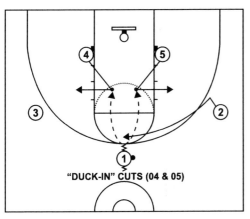

Diagram 4.5

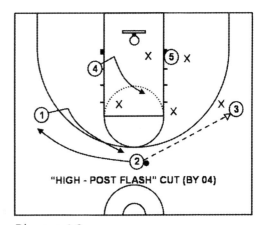

Diagram 4.6

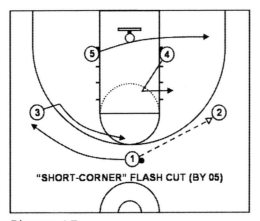

Diagram 4.7

Diagram 4.8 is another such option where the post on the side of the ball cuts to the short corner and is replaced by the opposite post, O4, using a gap cut (#19, #22). This option also attacks the interior of the defense from behind, while giving some freedom to the two post players. It gives the offense less predictability and distorts the zone defense (#2, #3, #4, #16, #22). This move creates a change in spot-up locations, which forces a change in what continuity offense is to be executed.

Diagram 4.9 could be a continuation of Diagram 4.8. O2 passes to O5, who had cut to the deep corner in Diagram 4.8. O2 cuts through the zone defense, possibly getting open on the cut, but more likely able to help O4 get open. O1 replaces O2, O3 replaces O1, (#19) and O2 then replaces O3 on the new weakside wing area.

Diagrams 4.10 and 4.11 both offer two more possible post options to the diamond continuity. O1 passes to O2 and exchanges with O3 (Diagram 4.10). Meanwhile, O5 has cut off O4's baseline pin screen. O4 can spin and seal his defender off as O5 cuts by to either the deep or the short corner (#16, #18, #24).

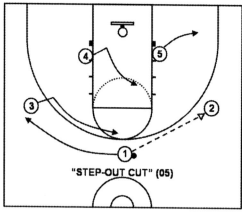

"STEP-OUT CUT" (O5)

Diagram 4.8

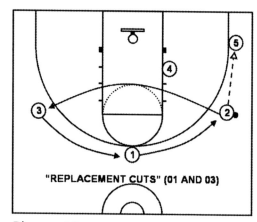

"REPLACEMENT CUTS" (O1 AND O3)

Diagram 4.9

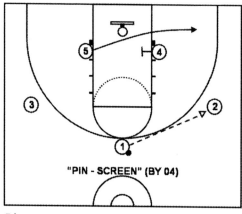

"PIN - SCREEN" (BY O4)

Diagram 4.10

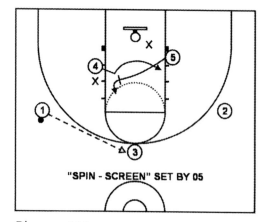

"SPIN - SCREEN" SET BY O5

Diagram 4.11

Diagram 4.11 shows a pass from a wing back to the point. When this pass occurs, the two post players can try to create a lob pass or a pass into the gap cut. By O5 back screening for O4, O4 could be open for the lob pass at the basket. O5 should immediately release from the screen and gap cut. Either O4 or O5 most likely will be open for a pass from O3 (#22, #23, #24).

Post entries are not the only one or two player options in the diamond continuity. The point guard has several options available, and when combined with the post options, the diamond continuity begins to look complex. Diagrams 4.12, 4.13, and 4.14 show the three dribble options from different positions on the court. Diagram 4.12 displays the gap dribble option, Diagram 4.13 the freeze dribble option, and Diagram 4.14 the pull-dribble option (#12).

Anytime a pass is made into the post players, the perimeter players try to find the gaps in the perimeter defense. They flare cut to those open gaps and get their feet and hands set for a possible pass from the post and a quick shot (#13, #21).

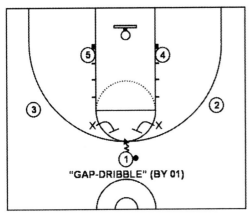

Diagram 4.12

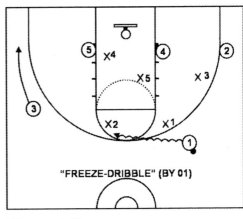

Diagram 4.13

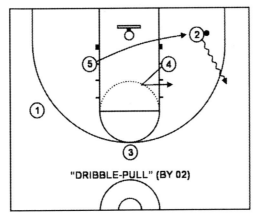

Diagram 4.14

Diamond Zone Offense's Continuity Rules

Entries from the split set, for example, fall easily into the spot-ups of the diamond zone offense continuity, after the ball has reached the wing area (via dribble or a pass). If any entry from the diamond zone offense doesn't result in a shot or a turnover, the ball should end up at the (new) ballside wing position. At the exact time that the entry/play out of the designated set is finished, the diamond continuity offense begins.

The ballside wing with the ball has five possible types of action with the ball:

- Shoot or shot fake (#13, #14)
- Drive or ball fake (#12, #13, #14)
- Make an inside pass to the ballside post (#21, #23)
- Make a skip pass to the weakside wing (#15)
- Reverse the ball at the top of the key (#9)

As the ballside wing passes the ball to a teammate, the rules of the diamond zone offense are initiated. Every one of these passes trigger action for all five offensive players to make their concerted series of movements that make up the diamond zone continuity.

If the ballside wing (O3 in Diagram 4.15) makes a skip pass to the opposite weakside wing (O1), that player receiving the skip pass looks to take a quick shot, to make an inside pass to the (new) ballside post player (O5) that is sealing off, or he looks to make a return skip-pass back where the first skip pass came from (O3) (#13, #15). The wings can throw skip passes to each other back and forth as many times as they wish, which could horizontally stretch the defense for them to protect the perimeter.

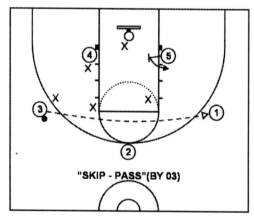

"SKIP - PASS"(BY O3)

Diagram 4.15

If the ballside wing (O1) makes a reversal pass to the top of the key (to O3), that triggers both post players to make reads on the defense, and consequently, the appropriate cuts they should make. The ballside post must read the defender on him.

An interior zone defender can play four different locations or positions against a ballside post:

- the frontside
- the three-quarter high side
- the three-quarter low side
- behind the post player

The diamond zone offense ballside post player (O4) makes the read on his defender and always makes his cut away from that post defender before going across the lane to the opposite low-post area. If the defender is playing on the low side or behind the ballside post, that post player could make a high duck-in cut away from the defender, but toward the passer, and continue across the lane to the opposite block position. The second option that the ballside post has is that if the defender 3/4 fronts or is directly in front, he could seal off the defender and make a low lob route cut and continue across the lane. Whatever method is chosen by the post defense, the continuity offense has a counter to it (#3).

While the ballside post (O4) reads the ballside post defense and makes the appropriate cut, the weakside post (O5) reads his teammate—the ballside post—and then makes the cut opposite the ballside post player's cut (while continuing across the lane). If the ballside post makes the high duck-in cut, the weakside post follows with the lob route. If the ballside post makes the low lob-route cut, the weakside post makes the high duck-in cut (#20, #22, #23, #24, #25).

The perimeter player at the top of the key should attack the defense via three different types of dribbles. The gap dribble gives the offense's four off-the-ball players operating against three defenders—a numerical advantage that should be beneficial to the offense (#3, #4, #12).

The freeze dribble places extreme pressure on the ball defender, while drawing the near defender toward him as well. This technique should prevent the original off-the-ball defender from being able to adequately cover the offensive player receiving the next pass (#3, #4, #12).

The pull dribble is used to tease more than one perimeter player as well as to draw the attention of inside zone defenders. The purpose of a pull dribble is to pull the defense in the direction of the perimeter dribble while then looking to throw back in the opposite direction of the pull dribble to the vacant area. The following explores more than just the one perimeter or two post options and looks at several special cuts of the diamond continuity (#3, #4, #12).

Options and Special Rules of the Diamond Zone Continuity Offense

The Short-Corner Cut

The ballside short-corner area has long been a weak area in many zone defenses, partially because of the confusion the area causes as to which player in the defense has that area (#3, #4). Diagram 4.16 illustrates a short-corner cut by O4 and the subsequent movement by the four other players. On the wing pass to O3 from O1, the new weakside post (O4) makes a cut from behind the defense to the new ballside short-corner, while the new ballside post (O5) shapes up strong and remains on the ballside block area, and the point (O1) flare cuts and exchanges with the weakside wing (O2), as he always does after making the wing pass (#16, #22, #24).

If no score develops from this cut, the ball is reversed to the opposite side of the floor, as demonstrated in Diagram 4.17 (#17). The new ballside block (O5) makes the same read on the ballside post defense and makes the appropriate cut (high or low) and crosses to the opposite side of the lane (#16, #22, #24). The original ballside short corner (O4) reads his teammate's cut, makes the opposite cut (low or high) towards the middle of the lane, but actually remains on the same side of the court in the mid-post area.

All five players are now back in the diamond zone offense spot-ups. Diagram 4.17 illustrates the appropriate cuts by the ballside post and the short corner when the post defense is playing on the high side or 3/4 fronting, while Diagram 4.18 is an example of the post defense playing on the low side. In this defense, O5 cuts away from the ballside post defender by ducking in toward the dotted circle (before ending up on the opposite side of the lane). The weakside post player (O4 in the short-corner area)

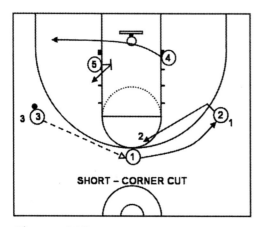

SHORT – CORNER CUT

Diagram 4.16

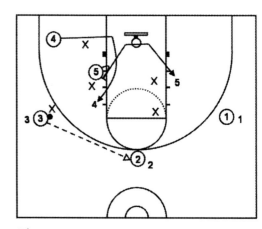

Diagram 4.17

makes the cut opposite of what O5 does by cutting low and then ending up on the low-post area on the same side (#3, #4, #16, #22, #24).

Once the new ballside wing (O1) receives the ball and he does not have a shot, a drive, an inside pass to the ballside post, or he does not reverse the ball to the new point (O2), the ballside wing could skip pass to the opposite weakside wing (O1). If the weakside wing receives the skip pass, he has several options that he could effectively use (Diagram 4.19). After receiving the skip pass, the weakside wing has the options that include:

- an immediate shot off of the skip-pass (#13, #14, #15)
- an inside pass to the (new) ballside block, who has sealed off the interior defender (#23, #24)
- a second skip-pass back to the original passer (#15)

That second skip-pass receiver then has the same three options to use. These options greatly stretch the zone defense horizontally, causing the defense to be weakened either on the inside, on the perimeter, or in both areas (#3, #4, #13, #15, #16).

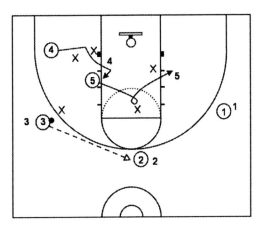

Diagram 4.18

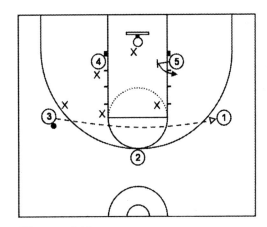

Diagram 4.19

Offensive Rebounding and Transition Responsibilities

Diagram 4.20 illustrates the assigned offensive rebounding and defensive transition out of any shots taken when running the diamond zone offense continuity. The three fullbacks attack the basket because they are the three best rebounders. The halfback becomes half rebounder and half defender because he is the fourth best rebounder. The tailback gets his "tail back" on defense to defend the basket (#8, #9).

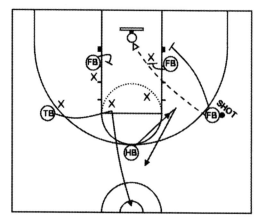

Diagram 4.20

Primary Fast Break into the Secondary Fast Break into the Diamond Continuity Offense

The offensive philosophy is such that the primary fast break and any full-court press offenses used must have a smooth transition into the secondary fast break. The secondary fast break must then have the compatibilities and the capabilities of flowing immediately into the diamond zone continuity. If you make a quick glance back to the fast break and secondary break discussions in Chapter 2, you will note the players are in spot-up locations consisting of two low post positions, two wing area positions, and one post area position when the secondary break ends. Therefore, there is no time taken to move personnel from the secondary break into the diamond zone continuity offense spot-ups. There can be an immediate beginning to this continuity (#1).

Entries/Plays into the Zone Offense

Entries/Plays from the Split Set

Entries are quick-hitters that attempt to score in just a matter of a few passes or other offensive actions, such as cutting, screening, or dribbling (#12, #18, #19, #22). Specific entries can also be developed and implemented to attack general weaknesses of a particular zone defense, as well as take advantage of specific offensive strengths that the entry/play could possibly possess (#3, #4, #5).

The split set is a symmetrical alignment that has a post player on both blocks, (O4 on the right and O5 on the left), a wing player on both wings (O2 on the right and O3 on the left), and the point guard (O1) centered up at the top of the key (Diagram 4.21). Even though these five positions are the same as the diamond zone continuity offense, the split set and its entries are not the same as the diamond continuity and its options. This set is how the entries begin, and the spot-ups the entries leave the personnel in are how the continuity begins.

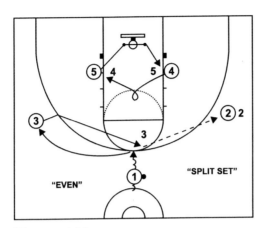

Diagram 4.21

After any entry has been executed and no shot or turnover takes place, the spot-ups of the diamond zone offense will have all five players in these continuity spot-ups. The spot-ups of the diamond zone offense are best when running against 2-3, 2-1-2, or 1-2-2 zone defenses.

If either entry fails in its attempt to score, all are designed to make sure that each of the five offensive players will end up in specific spot-up positions. If all five players find their spots, the offensive rebounding action and the defensive transition part of the zone offense should be at its peak efficiency (#7, #8). In addition, the zone offense can easily flow into the zone offense continuity from the spot-up positions, putting even more pressure on the opposition's defense. Each zone offensive set can offer as many different entries as the coaching staff and the players are comfortable with, which can make that offensive team a potentially better one. Each entry then should have the capabilities of being able to instantly flow into the diamond zone offense continuity.

Certain entries could also capitalize on opposing individual defender's defensive weaknesses, and/or could highlight and take advantage of individual offensive player's strengths (#5, #6). If a team can mentally handle several entries to incorporate into its zone offense package, the better the zone offense most likely will be. The more weapons a zone offense has, the more effective the offense is against the opposition.

Five entries that can be used out of the split set are described in the following sections, with each of the entries ending up in the spot-up positions of the diamond zone continuity. The first entry is called *even* (Diagram 4.21). Like four of the five mentioned entries, even is initiated by the point guard (O1), gap dribbling into the gap between the two defensive wings on top. When he is close enough to be able to make an inside-pass to either post player (O4 or O5), these two post players make their particular cuts, dependent upon the defensive play (#20, #22). On the even entry, the *even* man (O4) takes the *high* road and ducks in to the dotted circle, before going across to the opposite post position. Meanwhile, the odd man (O5) takes the low road by stepping toward the basket, before going across the lane to the opposite block position. If the point guard doesn't hit either post player, he passes the ball to either of the wings (O2 or O3) and then exchanges with the wing player who did not receive the pass. In Diagram 4.21, O1 passes to O2 and exchanges with O3. Both post players have actually exchanged post positions and end up on the opposite side of the lane from where they started. All five players are now in the proper spot-up positions for the diamond zone offense continuity to be utilized.

The second entry is an entry called *odd* and is identical to the even play, except the *odd* post player (O5) is the post player that takes the *high* cut, and the even post player (O4) takes the low cut (Diagram 4.22). Both post players again end up on the opposite mid-post position from where they started, while the three perimeter players have identical assignments and responsibilities as they have in the even play (Diagram 4.22). If a pass is made inside to either post, the three perimeter players flare cut to open spots for a kick-out pass and a passable shot (#20, #23).

Bam is the third entry and again is initiated by O1 gap dribbling into the gap between the two wings. In this entry, *both* post players duck in to the dotted circle, but both then drop back down to the same block position at which they started (Diagram 4.23) (#22, #24, #25). This entry causes an overload on the center of the defense, which makes it difficult for the zone defense to defend both post cutters (#2, #3, #4). As in both even and odd, if the point guard doesn't hit either post player, he passes the ball to either wing and then exchanges with the opposite wing player. As with all of the entries out of the split set after the initial wing pass, the entry is concluded. All five players are now in the proper spot-up positions for the diamond zone continuity (Diagram 4.23).

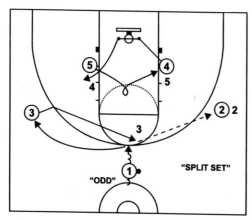

Diagram 4.22

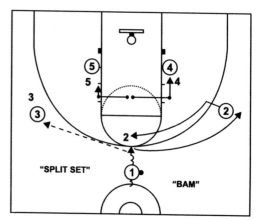

Diagram 4.23

A fourth entry called *push* is an entry initiated with O1 dribbling directly at an offensive wing on either side of the offense. Depending on the defensive alignment, this move could also be a freeze dribble (#12). In Diagram 4.24, O1 dribbles at the right wing and *pushes* that particular offensive wing (O2) to cut below both post players and across the lane to the opposite wing area. He replaces the opposite wing (O3) as that wing breaks to the top of the key to replace the point (#19). The original point (O1) has moved to the right wing on his dribble. This configuration moves all three of the perimeter players into three different perimeter spot-ups, which also causes the perimeter defenders to move. The two post players both stay at their original positions on the original dribble push, or they can execute any of the previous discussed moves (Diagram 4.25) (#22, #23, #24, #25). Once the ball is dribbled to the wing area and the point guard doesn't hit either post player, O1 either skip-passes the ball to the new weakside wing (O2) or reverses the ball to the top of the key (to O3) (#10, #15, #16). When O1 reverses the ball, only then do both post players duck in to the dotted circle from behind the line of defense through any seams and vacuums that are available (Diagram 4.25) (#16, #22, #23, #24, #25).

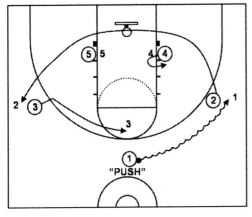

Diagram 4.24

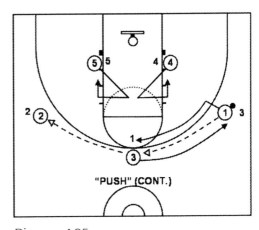

Diagram 4.25

On the catch, if the new point (O3 in this case) doesn't hit either post player ducking in, he passes the ball to either wing (in this case, O2 on the left or O1 on the right). The new point (O3) then exchanges with the wing, who did not receive the next wing pass (O1) (Diagram 4.25). At this point, the push entry is finished and the diamond zone continuity offense is ready to begin on the next pass by the wing.

Still another entry that can easily be run out of the 1-2-2 set is called *zoom* (when run to the left side of the court). This entry attacks the middle of the zone with both post players (O4 and O5) ducking in to the dotted circle and then returning to the mid-post on the same side of the court, while the point guard gap-dribbles at the two defensive wings. This action is identical to the bam entry, except the right wing (O2) cuts through behind the two post players ducking in and on to the opposite side's deep-corner area, while the other wing (O3) remains at his original position to receive the wing pass (Diagrams 4.26 and 4.27) (#12, #16, #22).

If the zone defense reacts to the duck-in cuts of both post players by stepping up with them as they cut, the cutting wing (O2 on zoom) can drift behind the backline of the defense and be open in the lane for a lob pass from O1 (#16, #17). The wing that remains at his particular wing area (O3 in Diagram 4. 26) should be ready to catch the wing pass, as does the cutting wing (O2) who should get himself ready to catch the down pass once he has finished his cut to the deep-corner (#13, #14). This cut moves the defensive perimeter players in the zone. If O1 doesn't hit either post player or hit the cutting wing for a lob pass (O2 in the zoom entry), O1 should hit the perimeter wing (O3) (Diagram 4.26). That wing looks to hit the new ballside corner (the opposite wing that cut through the lane and on to the opposite corner—O2 in this case). If the ball is down-passed to the deep corner and nothing develops, the ball is up passed from O2 to O3 and the ball is then reversed to O1 at the top of the key. On the reversal pass, both post players again make duck-in cuts in any available gaps near the dotted circle and eventually again drop back down to the same block positions. As these movements take place, the current ballside wing (O3 in Diagram 4.27) makes a cut to the basket, through the lane, and back out to the wing position, again, on the opposite side of the floor. The ballside corner (O2) then makes a replacement cut and fills the wing area just vacated by O3. O1 looks to hit O5 or O4 on their duck-in cuts, or to hit O3 for a lob pass on his cut behind the interior of the zone, or to hit O2 at the wing on his replacement cut, behind the perimeter of the zone (Diagram 4.27). These perimeter and interior cuts are constantly attacking various zone defenders from behind (#13, #16, #17, #19, #20, #21, #22, #23, #24, #25).

The *jet* entry is the same entry as the zoom entry, except that the entry is now passed (to O2) on the *right* side (Diagrams 4.28 and 4.29 for the jet entry and Diagrams 4.26 and 4.27 for the zoom entry).

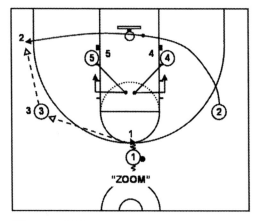

Diagram 4.26

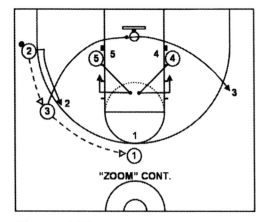

Diagram 4.27

The left entry (zoom) must be designated from the right entry (jet) for two reasons. It allows the designated wing, who has to cut to the basket, to get in motion earlier. Also, it gives coaches a chance to communicate from the bench the entry they think would be best for a particular defensive play, so that specific strengths of a particular offensive player might be capitalized and/or certain weaknesses of a particular defender might possibly be exploited (#2, #3, #4, #6).

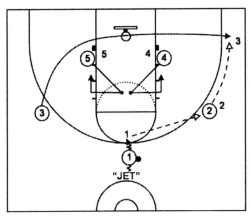

Diagram 4.28

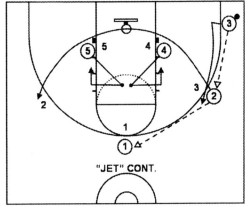

Diagram 4.29

Breakdown Drills for the
Diamond Zone Continuity Offense

Fundamental drills are presented in Chapter 7. They incorporate all the movements of the zone continuities. In this chapter (as in Chapters 3, 5, and 6), drills will be presented that teach the movements of this continuity as well as drills on fundamentals. So you should select drills from this chapter and from Chapter 7, if you wish to teach the diamond continuity zone offense.

Diagram 4.30 represents the first step in the diamond continuity: a pass from the point to the wing. The wing must be ready to shoot, drive, or pass again. In Diagram 4.30, R throws an outlet pass to P who passes to S for the shot (#10, #13, #14).

Diagram 4.31 drills on the gap dribble by the point guard, P, in the diagram. P passes to S who takes the shot. R rebounds and throws the outlet pass to P to continue this offensive drill (#10, #12, #13, #14).

Diagram 4.32 simulates the gap dribble by P and a duck-in cut by S. P passes to S who makes an inside move and shoots (#12, #16, #20, #21, #22, #23, #24, #25). R can be a dummy defender to provide resistance to S. R then rebounds all shots by S and again outlets the ball to P.

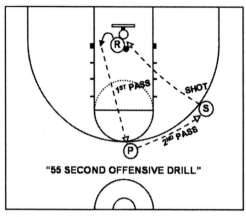

Diagram 4.30

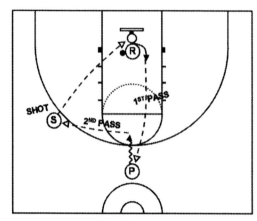

Diagram 4.31

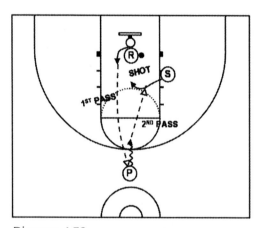

Diagram 4.32

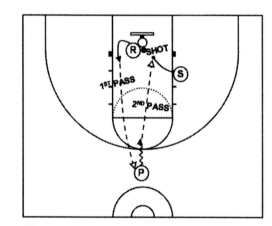

Diagram 4.33

Diagram 4.33 demonstrates P executing the gap dribble and S making a cut and going backdoor. P throws the lob pass to S for the score. Again, a rebounder executes the outlet pass if you choose to work on the fast break at the same time. If not, you players should move to defensive transition as each shot is taken (#12, #16, #20, #21, #22, #23, #24, #25).

Diagram 4.34 illustrates the wing guard cutting through the back of the zone (or the post player running the short corner entry in Diagram 4.7) and P receives an outlet pass (or a post pass while P is finding the open spot in the perimeter). P passes to the cutter in the short corner or the corner for the shot (#1, #12, #13, #14, #16). R rebounds and outlets the ball to P to continue the offensive drill.

Diagram 4.35 is the first to require decision making skills. O1 executes the gap dribble. O4 and O5 execute post entry moves and O1 passes to either for the shot. In this same format, you can work on Concept #20 from Chapter 1. This concept requires O4 or O5 to pass to O1 (#12, #20, #21, #22, #23, #24, #25).

Diagram 4.36 is a variation of Diagram 4.35. In this drill, you are working on the entire movement of the continuity, except the guard who would be cutting away from the initial pass. The manager passes to O3 while the post players are making one of their cuts (you can demand the cut you want the post players to work on). O3 then must pass to one of the post players. That post player can shoot or activate Concept #20. Diagram 4.37 is the same structure but the post players are executing a different set of cuts (#12, #20, #21, #22, #23, #24, #25).

Diagram 4.38 has a manager passing to O3. This pass simulates either the beginning of the diamond continuity by a pass to a wing, or the manager having penetrated with a gap dribble. O4 and O5 execute their movement when the ball is passed into the corner as the entry of Diagram 4.7. Instead of using O4, you could be

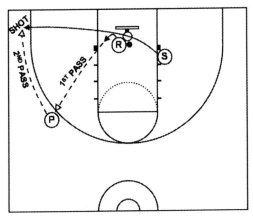

Diagram 4.34

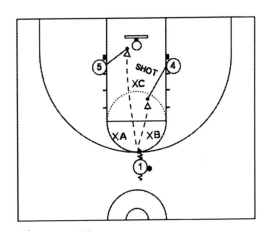

Diagram 4.35

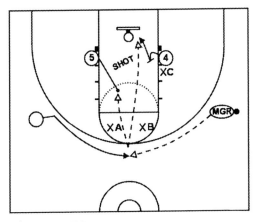

Diagram 4.36

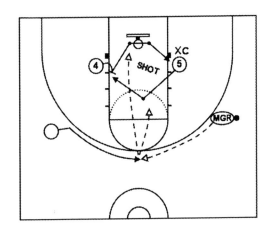

Diagram 4.37

drilling with the opposite wing, making this cut as in Diagram 4.24 (#10, #12, #13, #14, #15, #16, #17, #18, #19, #20, #21, #22, #23, #24, #25). O3 makes the pass to the cutter who then takes the deep-corner shot or passes to O5 for an inside shot. O5 rebounds the shot and then outlets the ball to the manager.

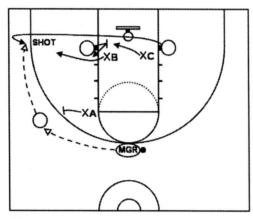

Diagram 4.38

Tape on the floor during preseason will help both post players and perimeter players learn and become accustomed to the high duck-in routes and the lob-cut routes that ballside post and weakside post players must make in the continuity scheme of the diamond zone offense. Place managers or other players in the drill to simulate post defenders and to illustrate their various defensive positions and locations when the ball is reversed (from the ballside wing to the point). Both post and perimeter players can learn and perfect the reads to make the appropriate cuts that need to be made for the offensive continuity to be successful. These drills could be used with and without a basketball. Diagrams 4.39 through 4.42 show the various defensive post

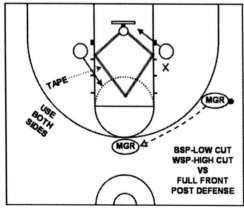

Diagram 4.39

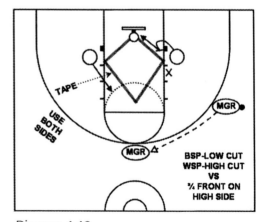

Diagram 4.40

player locations (#20, #21, #22, #23, #24, #25). Once the post player reads are thoroughly learned, the drill can be expanded by having a ball and the three perimeter players added to it (all concepts).

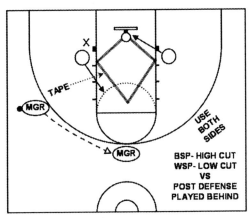

Diagram 4.41

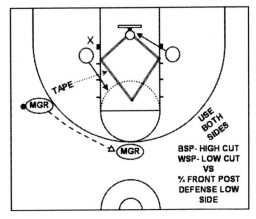

Diagram 4.42

Conclusion

This zone offense is fundamentally sound and applies many solid philosophies and concepts that can capitalize on many different zone defense's weaknesses, as well as utilizing the offense's own built-in strengths. Every phase of the game is clearly laid out as to what individual players have what specific responsibilities. Therefore, the offense is a carefully planned out zone offense that is efficient in every part of the game.

Having the flexibility of being able to use different alignments/sets allows this offense to attack various types of zone defenses that have even or odd fronts (i.e., 2-1-2 zones, 2-3 zones, 1-2-2 zones, 1-3-1 zones, and 1-1-3 zones). Once the ball is in the deep corner, most zones are pretty much the same in placement of their defensive personnel. With the diamond zone offense, you have the opportunity of being able to use different alignments/sets to initially attack the zone, as well as give the offense various cosmetic appearances at the beginning. This approach also gives the offense an important advantage of being able to use different entries/plays against the defenses, which makes it extremely difficult for the opposition to scout, prepare to defend against, and predict the offense. Having the opportunity of being able to use different sets and entries gives an offensive team two more distinct advantages. Each entry can be designed to take advantage of individual player's specific offensive strengths. This advantage also gives the offense an opportunity to capitalize on particular individual opponent's defensive weaknesses or that particular zone defense's weaknesses in general.

Yet with the flexibility and multiple options that the diamond zone offense possesses, it remains a simple one for the offensive players to be able to perform. With each position being a specialized position, each position player clearly knows his responsibilities and assignments. By using the many different breakdown drills, each position player can sharpen his offensive skills and be able to perform them at a high degree of efficiency. Developing and utilizing breakdown drills for each position gives players an excellent vehicle in improving their basketball skills in addition to learning that specific position's responsibilities and assignments. This zone offense overall continually improves as a whole as each individual player improves in his overall comprehension of the offense, as well as the specific offensive skills that are required for the offense to be successful. The offense becomes more and more efficient with its use—both from practice and also from the actual games. As the offense becomes more and more productive and efficient, it can also serve as a great benefit to the overall team's defense by becoming more proficient in not reducing turnovers and missed shots, but also in the team performance of its defensive transition and ball control effectiveness.

5

The Heavy and Rotation Zone Continuity Offenses

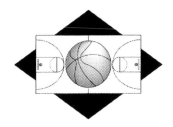

Introduction to the Rotation Zone Continuity Offense

The rotation zone offense and the heavy zone offense are two different zone offense continuities that have odd fronts and that are both very effective against even front zone defenses (such as a 2-1-2 or a 2-3 zone). Both can also be effective against a 1-2-2 zone. The spot-ups of these two continuities are slightly different: heavy continuity offense (Diagram 5.1) uses a short corner and a mid to low post to distort the defense, while the rotation continuity offense (Diagram 5.2) uses a low-post player who breaks into the corner, a high to midpost player, and a wing cutter (#3, #4, #17, #19, #22).

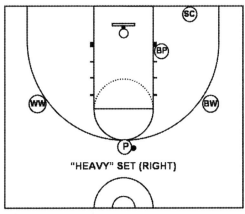

Diagram 5.1

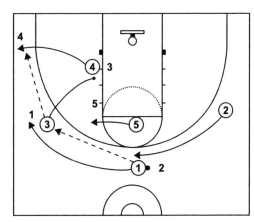

Diagram 5.2

Many different entries from different offensive alignments can work well with and can flow into either continuity attack. The two attacks are interchangeable by simply having the low-post break to the short corner (heavy) or to the corner (rotation) (#2, #3, #4, #5). Breaking to the deep corner would then dictate that the wing that made the pass to the deep corner should then rotate through the defense to the wing on the opposite side of the court and run the rotation continuity zone offense (#19).

A team's offensive scheme can be set up so that it can have multiple secondary fast breaks, and if the secondary fast break does not produce transition points, each secondary break utilized must be then able to flow directly into the heavy or the rotation continuities (#1). If scoring does not result from the entries out of possible various sets, the five players should end up in the spot-ups of one or the other zone offense continuity that will allow the offense to continue attacking the opposition. This strategy keeps the zone offense in a continuous attack mode, preventing the opposition's defense from recovering or relaxing (#26). The heavy and rotation continuities will flatten out the zone defense on one side of the floor and allows for players to make basket cuts (with cuts both on the perimeter and in the post) (#15, #16, #17, #18, #19, #20, #21, #22, #23, #24, #25).

Placement of Personnel of the Rotation Zone Continuity Offense

The rotation zone offense continuity is a good offense to use when the team has only one strong post player and four good perimeter players. The threat of good perimeter shooting from four different perimeter spots really stretches the zone defense, weakening the defensive interior for the lone post player in the offense (#4, #10).

With the standard numbering system, O1 should be the point guard, O2 should be the big guard, O3 is the small forward, O4 is more of a second small forward, and O5 is the center. While O2 and O3 should be good ballhandlers and shooters, O1 should be the best ballhandler and interior passer. O4 should be the best perimeter shooter from the baseline, where he basically will roam from corner to corner as the ball is swung from side to side (#5, #9).

It is extremely important that all four of the perimeter players be outstanding passers and good perimeter shooters. If they are not outstanding perimeter shooters, they must at least appear to be offensive threats from the perimeter. They must look like they will take the perimeter shots every time they catch the basketball (#10, #12, #13, #14, #15, #17).

It is very important that all perimeter players know the various types of zone dribbles and passes and how to utilize all of them effectively at the appropriate times in the attempt to both vertically and horizontally stretch the defense. Doing so weakens the defense and allows the offense to be able to probe the weakened interior of the zone defense (#10, #12, #16, #17, #21, #22, #23, #24, #25).

The one offensive post player must be able to catch the various types of passes made to him on the interior and also have a variety of post moves to be able to effectively score inside. He must be able to read the defense, particularly the interior defense, and know how to gap cut (#20, #21, #22, #23, #24, #25).

Spot-up Locations and Descriptions

The spot-ups for the rotation zone offense continuity are somewhat different than the spot-ups of other zone continuity offenses. The basic spot-up positions are defined with the location of the ball being the ballside and the opposite side being called the weakside or the offside. The spot-ups are set up in an odd front alignment having a point, a ballside wing, a weakside wing, a ballside post, and a ballside corner. The point position is centered at the top of the key (just outside the three-point line). The ballside wing and a weakside wing are located on the free-throw line extended (an imaginary line), just outside the three-point line, on both sides of the court. The ballside post position is always on the ballside, and initially starts at the tight elbow area, which is in the high-post area.

After he makes his replacement cut, the ballside post ends up on the first notch above the low-post block. The corner perimeter position is always on the ballside, initially in the low post, before stepping out to the ballside deep corner just outside the three-point line and a step off the baseline.

Using Diagrams 5.2 and 5.3, the entire rotation zone offense continuity can be explained and the various passes can be seen. In Diagram 5.2, O1 passes to O3 who passes to O4 in the corner. O3 begins his cut by stopping only for a moment at the low

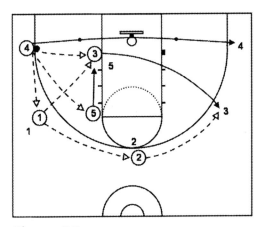

Diagram 5.3

post. O5 rolls to the high post. O1 then replaces O3 (#17, #19). These moves create a box overload to start the passing entries. O2 rotates to the top of the key to replace O1.

Diagram 5.3 shows all these possible passes and cuts. O4 can pass inside to O3 at the low block or pass inside to O5 at the high or midpost (#17, #19, #20, #21). O4 can skip pass to O2 (#15) or skip it to O3 on the new weakside wing. After O3 quickly empties out and cuts through, O5 then slides down to post up. O4 looks to then hit O5.

O4 can pass back out to O1. This pass keys O4 to cut along the baseline to the far corner or O3 to cut to the weakside wing (#10, #11, #12, #13, #14, #15, #16, #17). O1 can now pass inside to O5 (#20, #21, #22, #23, #24, #25) or reverse the ball to O2 or O3 (#10). O1 could throw the skip pass to O3 (#15). The rotation continuity is now ready to be run to the other side of the court.

Diagram 5.4 illustrates the possible passes now open from the other side of the court. O2 can swing the ball to O3 and on to O4. On that down pass, O3 cuts through and posts up momentarily before emptying out. As O3 exits, O5 gap cuts to post up on the new ballside block. O1 and O2 rotate over after O3 starts the chain reaction of perimeter cuts (#19, #22).

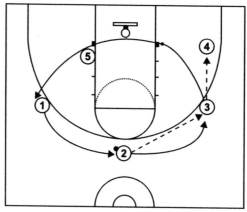

Diagram 5.4

Entries and Special Options of the Rotation Zone Continuity Offense

Diagram 5.5 shows the basic post cuts as the ball is reversed. O5 cuts from low post to high post to low post as the ball is passed from corner to corner. O4 runs the baseline to receive the pass in both corners. O5 times his cuts, trying to find the gap in the interior of the zone defense (#19, #22).

If O4 is also capable of handling inside duties, coaches could run the X cut. In the X cut, O5 would follow the pass around and then cut to the corner to receive the pass from O2. O4 would cut into the low-post area on his pass to O1 (Diagram 5.5). Then O4 would follow O5's cut out of the high post with a cut into the high post on another reversal pass from O3 to O2 (#22).

The next concepts discussed are the dribbling concepts and techniques. Diagram 5.6 shows the gap dribble by O1. If both of the front defenders in the 2-1-2 zone defense cover O1, O1 can pass to either wing. If the pass is made to O2, he has an immediate shot, pass, or dribble (#12, #13, #14). If XE comes out to cover O2, the pass inside to O4 gets a lay-up. If XC tries to come from the post, the pass inside to O5 opens up (#3, #4).

Diagram 5.7 illustrates the freeze dribble being run by O2. O2 dribbles directly toward XA. XB covers the dribble, but XA must stay in support, which opens the pass

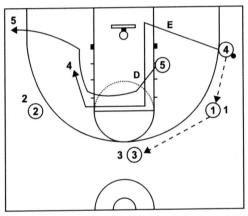

Diagram 5.5

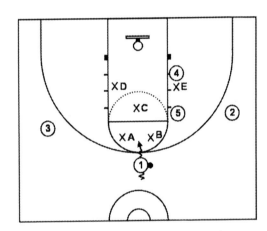

Diagram 5.6

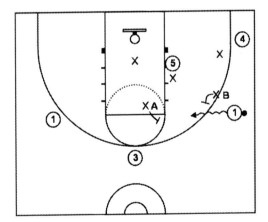

Diagram 5.7

to O1 or O3 for the quick perimeter shot (#12, #13, #14). O4 and O5 could be making their cuts of the continuity, and either pass to O1 or O3 would open up all kinds of inside passing options (previously discussed), depending on how the defense slides (#16, #17, #19, #20, #21, #22, #23, #24, #25).

Diagram 5.8 demonstrates the pull dribble being used by O4. The diagram begins with O2 already having passed into the corner and cut to the low block (Diagram 5.3). Now O4 pulls his defender out, while O2 makes a move as if to cut to the opposite side, (as in the rotation continuity) before breaking back to the short corner or the deep corner for a pass from O4 and an easy shot. This cut and replace maneuver by O4 and O2 also has O5 replacing O2 on the ballside low post (#19). If O4 passes to O2, he can cut through the zone to the other side, as the continuity calls for, and O4 and O2 have simply exchanged duties. This move opens up all the options discussed in Diagrams 5.2 through 5.4.

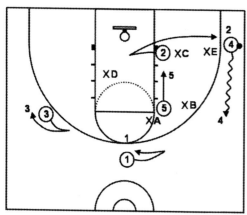

Diagram 5.8

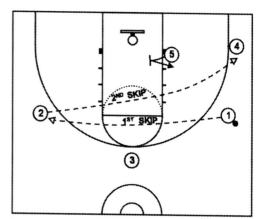

Diagram 5.9

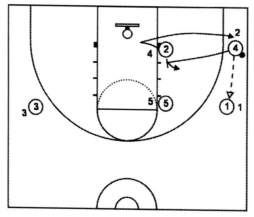

Diagram 5.10

Diagram 5.9 displays a double skip pass for a perimeter shot for the corner player and a screen by O5. If the defense is sliding quickly from side to side as the ball moves from side to side, the offense can skip pass to one side then skip pass back for an easy perimeter shot (Diagram 5.9). O1 skip passes to O2 and the defense races for positioning on the opposite side of the court. O2 skip passes back to O4 who has received a baseline pin-screen from O5 (#10, #13, #14, #15, #18). O4 can either take a perimeter shot, make an inside pass to O5, or even make another skip pass back to O2 (#13).

Diagram 5.10 exhibits another way to use a baseline screen. After O2 has passed to O4 to begin the continuity, O2 cuts to the low post (Diagram 5.2). O4 passes back out to O1 and goes to pin screen for O2, who cuts to the corner for the perimeter shot (#13, #14). O2 has a possible shot, an inside pass opportunity to O4, an up pass to O1, or a skip pass to O3 on the weakside wing. This option quickly and unexpectedly overloads the zone defense, both on the interior as well as on the perimeter, with the offense only having to find the opening (#3, #4).

Offensive Rebounding and Transition Responsibilities

Coaches should have clear-cut offensive rebounding responsibilities for all five of the offensive players in the zone offense (#8). When the shot is missed, all three fullbacks and the halfback must overload the weakside of the zone with rebounders so as to outnumber the opposition and overload the area where the majority of missed shots will fall (#3, #4, #5). If no offensive rebound is secured, offensive players are in position to immediately execute the defensive fast break (Diagram 5.11) (#7). The rebounding techniques are the same as have already been discussed in Chapters 3 and 4. Diagram 5.11 shows the movements out of the spot-up positions in the rotation continuity into the offensive rebounding and defensive transition.

Primary Fast Break into the Secondary Fast Break into the Rotation Zone Continuity Offense

The primary fast break into the secondary break was discussed in Chapter 2. To get from the secondary break into the spot-up positions of the rotation continuity, O4 would merely go to the high post, while O5 would chase the ball and go to the newly declared ball low post, if he does not receive the pass from the wing (O1) on the right or the O3 on the left. If O5 is not open, he should step out into the deep corner on the ballside to become the probable option for the wing. Receiving that pass initiates the wing cutting through the block and on through to the opposite wing area. This play is illustrated in a similar manner in the following discussion. All the other attackers are already in their spot-up positions when the secondary break ends.

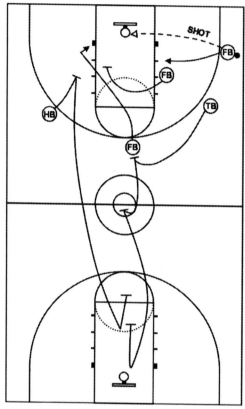

Diagram 5.11

Alignments/Sets into the
Rotation Zone Continuity Offense

The alignments/sets of this zone offense are very important to the overall zone offense package (as are the entries/plays). Regardless of the sets/alignments and of the plays/entries that are run, all must end in the zone offense continuity spot-ups, so that the continuity offense can stay in effect. Particular areas of the zone defense that need to be exploited—because of the zone defense's weaknesses, specific weaknesses of individual defenders, or because of the specific players' individual strengths—can only be attacked if initially set up in certain zone offense sets/alignments (#2, #3, #4).

All the sets and continuities are interchangeable. The sets of Chapter 3 can easily evolve into the sets in Chapter 4, this chapter, or the next, with only one player having to move. This adaptability permits the offense to operate most entries into most spot-ups for the different continuities, making the three principles available: same entries, different sets; different entries, different sets; and different entries, same set (#6).

The even and odd plays are run out of the split set. They end up in the spot-ups for the diamond zone continuity offense. The good and bad plays are identical because they too are initiated out of the split set, but these entries flow into the rotation zone continuity offense. The following is an example of one play out of the split set evolving into the spot-ups of another continuity. Diagram 5.12 shows the change from the split set (1-2-2) into the rotation continuity spot-ups (1-3-1). In the split set, O1 penetrates the gap. On the *good* play, O4 ducks-in and O5 goes low. O4 and O5 run their inside cuts of the even play (Chapter 4). However, O4 cuts to the high post area and stays as the pass is made from O1 to O2. O1 exchanges with O3, as is required in the even play.

Now, however, the offense is in the rotation spot-ups for the rotation continuity offense. O5 can break out to the corner and O2 can pass to him. O2 could then cut through the zone defense, as is required in the rotation continuity (Diagram 5.13). The offense has changed from the diamond continuity to the rotation continuity using the gap entry.

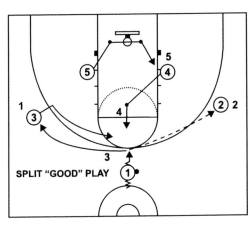

Diagram 5.12

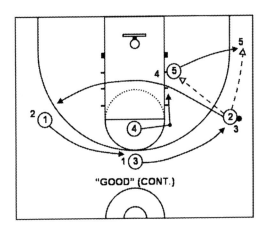

Diagram 5.13

Other Entries

Diagram 5.14 exhibits the play called *bad* (opposite of even is odd, opposite of good is bad) into the rotation continuity using an exchange by two perimeter players: O5 is the player that ducks-in and O4 goes low. O1 gap dribbles and passes to O3 (#12). O1 and O2 immediately exchange. This exchange puts O1 back at the point guard position when O3 passes to the corner and cuts through the defense (running the continuity), with O2 replacing O3. Coaches may want to use this play when the team you are playing against is an exceptional fast break team and O1 is your tailback.

Diagrams 5.15 and 5.16 offer an entry (called ron) that allows O1 to be the point guard, bringing the ball up the court, and also becoming the wing that cuts through the defense as the continuity is being run. Diagram 5.15 shows O2 setting a screen for O1 (#18). This screen could possibly result in an immediate shot by either O1 or O2 at the top of the key; or, it could result in O1 penetrating into the heart of the zone defense with a dribble (Diagram 5.15).

If neither develops because of good defense, Diagram 5.16 shows O1 passing to O5, who has stepped out to the deep corner, and O1 cutting through the zone defense. O1 brings the ball up the court, sets up the offense, and becomes the potential shooter, both inside and on the perimeter. This involvement of O1 is Concept #6 in action: capitalize on your offensive personnel's individual strengths via entries into your continuities.

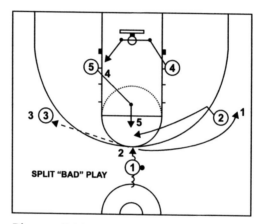

Diagram 5.14

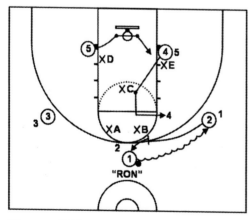

Diagram 5.15

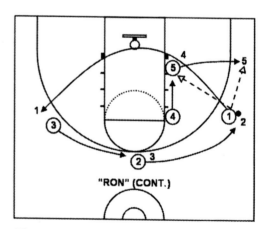

Diagram 5.16

Entries Out of a Stack Set That Flow Into the Rotation Continuity Offense

An outstanding entry that can be run out of the stack set is described in the sections that follow. Each of the four possibilities of this entry will end up in the spot-up positions of the rotation zone offense, which will allow the offense to continually flow for an indefinite period of time. Doing so keeps the zone offense constantly in an attack mode and prevents the opposition from scoring because they must stay on defense (#26).

Diagram 5.17 illustrates the stack alignment/set and an entry called *chase*, when the ball is passed to O2 and all players end up in the spot-ups of the rotation zone offense. The chase entry fittingly involves the two post players *chasing* the ball to the new ballside after the first wing pass is made. This play is initiated by O1 gap dribbling into the gap between the two defenders at the top of the zone. The even man (O4) takes the high road and ducks in to the dotted circle, while the odd man (O5) takes the low route. If the point guard doesn't hit either post player, he passes the ball to either wing. Both post players then *chase* the wing pass by following the ball and posting up on whatever side is the new ballside. O4 goes to the ballside high-post area and O5 goes to the ballside low post and quickly on to the ballside corner area after he makes a step-out cut.

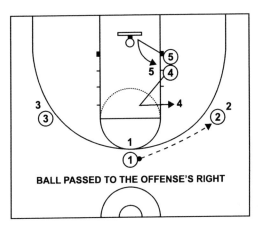

BALL PASSED TO THE OFFENSE'S RIGHT

Diagram 5.17

This entry initially puts pressure on the defense's middle interior and then raises questions to the defense on who is to cover the corner area with the ball in the wing area. A great deal of offensive unpredictability is created for the defense, because even the offense does not know which side the wing pass will be made to, and therefore, which side the post players and the eventual corner player will end up. Diagrams 5.21 through 5.23 illustrate the chase entry when the ball is passed to the right wing (O2), while Diagrams 5.18 through 5.20 show the same *chase* entry with the point guard (O1) passing the ball to the wing (O3) on the left side (#2, #4, #12, #22).

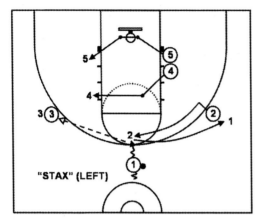

Diagram 5.18

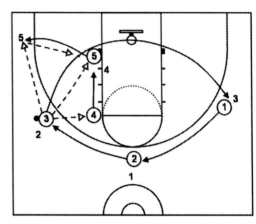

Diagram 5.19

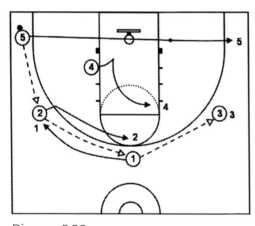

Diagram 5.20

Diagram 5.21

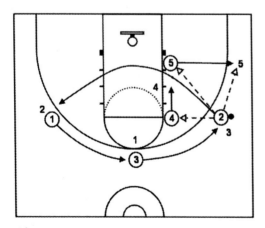

Diagram 5.22

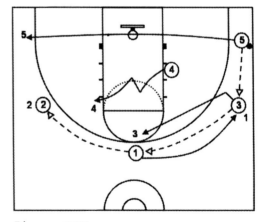

Diagram 5.23

After the wing pass, O1 exchanges with the wing player who did not receive the pass by making a flare cut. After the low-post player (O5) briefly posts up, he makes a step-out cut to become the new ballside corner. This move opens up the options of the ballside wing with the ball to be able to make a down pass immediately followed by that player's basket cut (O3) and the two other perimeter players' replacement cuts (O1 and O2 in Diagram 5.19 with O1 and O3 in Diagram 5.22).

All five players are now in the proper spot-up positions for the rotation zone offense continuity to be continued, with O4 always the high-post player who slides down the lane after the down pass and basket cut. O5 always is the offensive player who ends up in the deep-corner area, with O1, O2, and O3 always being at the two wing positions and the point position (Diagrams 5.20 and 5.23). This specialization makes every player knowledgeable of his responsibilities and more proficient in the skills needed for success (#5).

Breakdown Drills for the
Rotation Zone Continuity Offense

Shooting drills, passing and catching drills, screening and cutting drills, offensive rebounding drills, and defensive transition drills are types of drills that can be created to improve the many facets and fundamentals of the rotation zone offense. Shooting drills, featuring the 55-second structure, are offered in Chapter 7. More important are drills concerned with teaching the movements of the heavy and the rotation continuities.

Shooting drills should also have passers (also under some form of pressure) that are making the same type of passes from the same locations that would take place in games. Diagrams 5.24 through 5.31 show the 55-second shooting/offense drills for all five of the player positions in the rotation zone offense in their particular areas where they will shoot the majority of their shots.

The spots where they will catch the ball from in games is also included in these shooting drills, as well as the spots where they could start (before they make their specific cut to the ball). The illustrations are on just one side of the floor, but should be mirrored with the passer and the shooter on the opposite sides of the floor as the diagrams. Remember that every one of the 55-second shooting/offense drills are drills that should have the proper techniques emphasized (by the coaching staff) not only of the shooters, but for every player involved.

Diagram 5.24 displays the corner to wing passing options. Diagram 5.25 offers the wing to point passing options. Diagram 5.26 illustrates the wing-to-wing skip pass

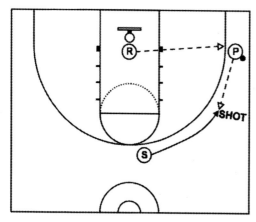

Diagram 5.24

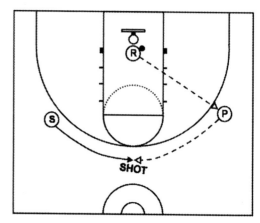

Diagram 5.25

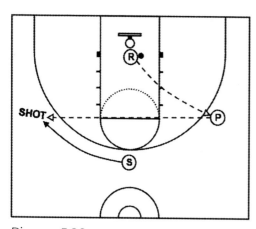

Diagram 5.26

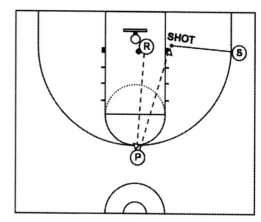

Diagram 5.27

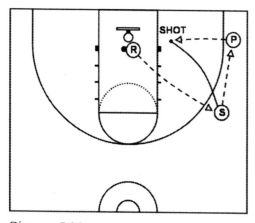

Diagram 5.28

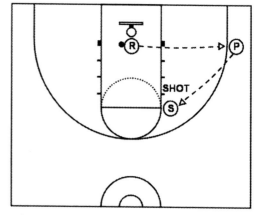

Diagram 5.29

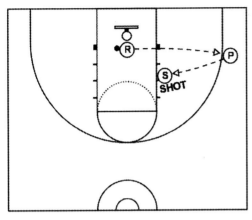

Diagram 5.30

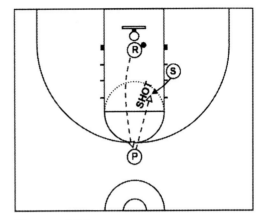

Diagram 5.31

maneuvers. Diagram 5.27 displays the point to low post lob pass. Diagram 5.28 drills on the wing to corner options. Diagram 5.29 exhibits the corner to high post options, and Diagram 5.30 displays the corner to low post options. Diagram 5.31 is another point to low post cutting option.

Diagram 5.32 illustrates the gap dribble option as well as the wing to post options. This drill involves all five players. O2 reverse passes to O1 (#10). O1 gap dribbles (#12) and has the option to pass to either post players (#20, #21, #22, #23, #24, #25); or, he can pass to O3 (#13, #14, #15). O3 then has the options to pass to the high post or to the low post. Two balls are used on this last option: place one ball at the feet of O3 and let the pass from O1 to O3 be the other ball. On the first ball, O3 throws the lob pass to O5 as he cuts behind the defense (#16), and on the second ball, O3 passes to O4 at the high or midpost (#20, #21, #22, #23, #24, #25). Obviously, both pass receivers catch the pass and shoot the ball at game speeds.

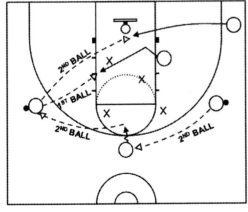

Diagram 5.32

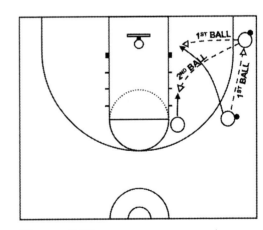

Diagram 5.33

Diagram 5.33 involves only the high post, the ballside wing, and the corner. All the options of these three are covered. O2 passes to O5 and cuts to the low post. O5 hits O2 for the inside pass and an inside move for a shot. O5 can also pass to O4 at the midpost or the low post for his inside options (#20, #21, #22, #23, #24, #25). A second ball could be placed at O5's feet so both O2 and O4 can take shots in this drill.

Introduction to the Heavy Zone Offense

This chapter is an ideal example of having two similar, yet different zone offense continuities. Each has its own distinct entity with similar yet still different spot-up locations for the offensive personnel. Each can start in the same initial offensive alignments/sets such as the split set or the stacks set. Each continuity offense can have very similar entries/plays that utilize offensive skills in similar manners and attack defenses in similar ways. The names of the entries are different because those entries, however similar, belong to a particular family—the zone offensive continuity family. A good example is that both the rotation zone offense continuity and the heavy zone offense continuity have entries out of the split set where O4 is the designated post player that ducks in to the middle of the lane while O5 steps towards the basket. Both post players follow the wing pass and end up on the new ballside. In the *good* play, the lower of the two post players (O5 in this example) posts up and then makes a step-out cut to the deep corner on the ballside so that the rotation continuity offense can instantly be executed. The *you* play looks very similar and attacks the defense in the same manner, with the same cuts, but O5 then steps out to the short-corner area (instead of the deep-corner area) so that the heavy continuity offense can immediately begin and continue the attack on the opposition. Both offenses have somewhat different passing rules and cuts, but have the same offensive rebounding and defensive transition assignments (#7, #8). So the two continuity offenses still have their own separate identities and characteristics.

Placement of Personnel

For the heavy zone offense continuity to be especially effective, all three of the perimeter players (O1, O2, and O3) should be outstanding perimeter shooters, especially off of the pass. Stretching the opposition's zone defense both vertically and horizontally helps allow the offense to probe the inside of the zone defense. It is also a necessity that all three perimeter players know the types of zone dribbles and passes and how they can effectively use all of them at the appropriate times (#5, #12, #13, #14).

The two post players (most likely O4 and O5) must be able to especially read the interior post defense. They also must be able to work well together and be able to read each other's interior cuts. They must be able to catch all types of passes made to them on the interior as well as be able to effectively score inside. A coaching staff must carefully evaluate the players' skills and then make the appropriate offensive position assignments (#5, #22, #24, #25).

Spot-up Locations and Descriptions

The spot-ups for this particular heavy zone offense continuity are similar but are somewhat different than the spot-ups of the rotation zone offense continuity previously described. The similarities are that the three perimeter spot-up positions are identical in both the heavy and the rotation zone offense continuities. The one unique position is the short-corner position that exists only in the heavy zone offense instead of the deep corner position that exists only in the rotation zone continuity offense. It is always located on the ballside, a step off the baseline, midway between the block and the sideline. The ballside post position is anywhere from the first notch above the ballside low-post block to the ballside high-post area. This spot is slightly higher than the ballside low-post position of the rotation zone offense continuity spot-up position because of the spacing difference of the short corner's spot-up location used in the heavy zone offense continuity spot-up. When a weakside post position for this particular zone offense presents itself, it is located on the first notch above the weakside block (Diagrams 5.34 and 5.35).

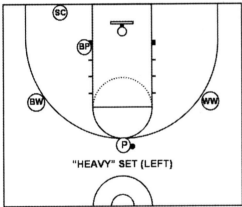

Diagram 5.34

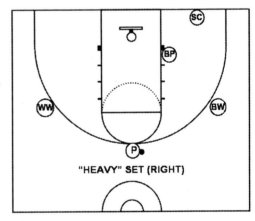

Diagram 5.35

Heavy Zone Offense's Continuity Rules

The rules of the heavy zone offense continuity are based on specific passes to players in specific locations (#5). Seven passes can be made within the heavy zone offense continuity and each pass results in a different series of movements made by the four off-the-ball offensive players. Each pass dictates fundamentally sound movement and action by the offensive team. The seven passes are shown in Diagrams 5.36 (A through D) and 5.37 (E through G):

A. Wing pass (O1 to O2) (#13)

B. Inside pass (O1 to O4 or O2 to O4) (#23)

C. Short-corner pass (O2 to O5) (#4, #13)

D. Outside pass (O4 to O2 or O4 to O1) (#13, #21)

E. Up pass (O5 to O2) (#13)

F. Reversal pass (O2 to O1) (#9, #13)

G. Skip pass (O2 to O3) (#13, #15)

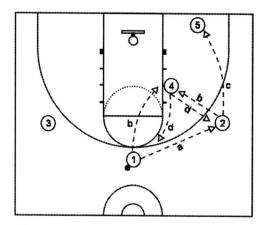 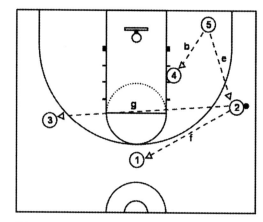

Diagram 5.36   Diagram 5.37

Whenever a wing pass is made (from the point area), the passer makes a flare cut exchange to the opposite wing area, while that wing makes a replacement cut to the point area. This action is simply the two off-the-ball perimeter players switching positions, but the switching should be done in a specific manner. The proper technique allows both players the opportunity to not only be able to receive the ball, but to be able to effectively do something productive with the ball on the return pass (#11). In this illustration in Diagram 5.38, O1 makes a wing pass to O2. O3 makes a replacement cut to the top of the key, while O1 makes a flare cut to the weakside wing area. O1 and O3 have simply exchanged locations, but have done so in a manner that places both of them as scoring threats in the zone offense (#9) (Diagram 5.38).

Anytime an inside pass is made, the short-corner player who did not receive the pass, instantly dive-cuts to the basket for scoring opportunities. In this example, O1 is the ballside wing who makes the inside pass to O4. The short corner (O5 in this case) dives to the basket (#22). If he does not receive the pass, he looks immediately to become an offensive rebounder on the weakside post area. The passing ballside wing

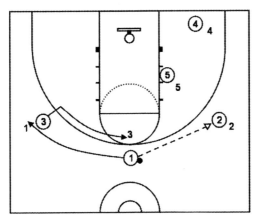

Diagram 5.38

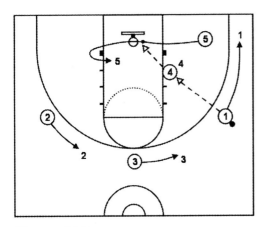

Diagram 5.39

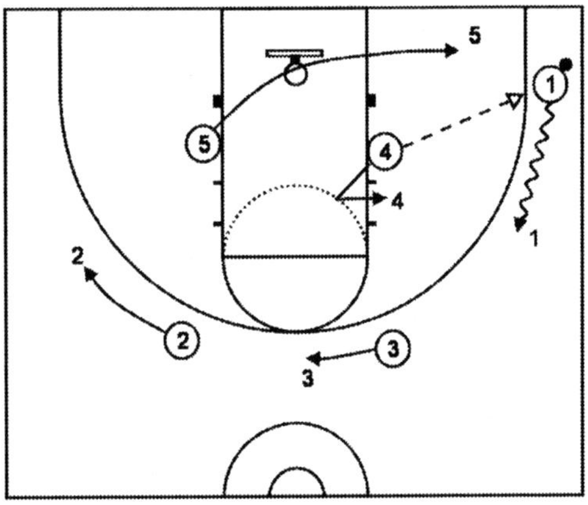

Diagram 5.40

(O1) makes a flare-cut to the ballside deep corner, while the two other off-the-ball perimeter players (O2 and O3) rotate toward the ball near the two elbow areas. Here, O1, O3, and O2 all make the flare-cuts on the perimeter, helping the post player with the ball to combat the defense's double-team attempt on the ball when it is passed inside (#21). If the action does not result in a shot being taken, the ball is outside-passed back to the ballside wing area (O1). When that wing (O1) has no jump shot, he makes a pull-dribble up from the deep-corner back to his original wing area, the new weakside post (O5) works on making a cut back to his original short corner area, while the ballside post (O4) makes a duck-in cut through the lane and returns to the original ballside block area (Diagrams 5.39 and 5.40).

Anytime a short-corner pass (from O2 to O5 in the diagrams) is made, the post player (O4) instantly dive-cuts to the basket for scoring opportunities. If he does not receive the pass, he looks immediately to become a potential offensive rebounder in

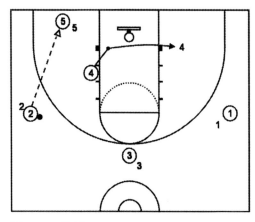

Diagram 5.41

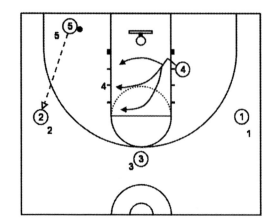

Diagram 5.42

the weakside post area. If the ball returns to the ballside wing (O2) via an up-pass (from O5), the new weakside post (O4) makes a gap cut through the lane and returns to his original spot back in the ballside post area (Diagrams 5.41 and 5.42) (#22). The action is illustrated on the left side of the floor to demonstrate that the offense must be used on both the left and the right side of the court.

Whenever the action is stalled on one side of the floor, the offense must reverse the ball to probe for inside or perimeter weaknesses of the defense's other side. This search may be done by either making reverse passes or skip passes. Both are effective passes when the action dictated by these passes is implemented (#15).

When the ball is reversed from the ballside wing to the perimeter player at the top of the key in the point area, both inside players (the ballside post and the short-corner) have one simple rule (#5). They both automatically make their x-cuts (#22). In the heavy zone offense, an x-cut is both post players making gap cuts in any route across and through the lane to the opposite side of the floor before ending up exchanging their original inside positions. The original short corner (O4) becomes the ballside post on the new ballside, while the original ballside post (O5) becomes the new short corner on the new ballside of the court. This movement is effective because the zone defense is constantly reacting to the basketball and the ball has just been reversed. This distraction leaves specific players forgotten and unseen, behind the backline of the zone defense. Therefore, these players are potentially lethal to the defense (#9, #16).

The original ballside post players (O4 and O5) are suddenly behind the zone defense and out of the defenders' sight because their focus in a zone defense is the basketball. The two original ballside post players are not seen and have now momentarily been forgotten by the defense (#16).

The perimeter player with the ball at the top of the key (O3) should retain the ball and carefully look inside for either x-cutter (Diagram 5.43). If the point passes to one of the x-cutters, the previously mentioned rules concerning inside passes or short corner passes with the appropriate off-the-ball movement (Diagrams 5.44 and 5.45) (#21, #23). If neither is open, the new point (O3) can continue the ball-reversal and make a wing pass in that same direction (to O1) then make the flare-cut exchange (with O2) (#9). Everyone is in the proper spot-ups for the heavy zone offense to continue (Diagram 5.46) (#26).

The other scenario is that the new point (O3) can make the wing pass back to the side where the first reversal pass came from (to O2). This pass becomes not only a wing pass but also a reversal pass. Therefore, the two off-the-ball perimeter players (O3 and O1) make another flare-cut exchange and the two inside players (O4 and O5) make their second x-cut (back to the new ballside) (Diagram 5.47). Organized movement by the offense ensues for the defense to contend with. Defensive weaknesses can be discovered and then attacked with this simple series of passes (#3).

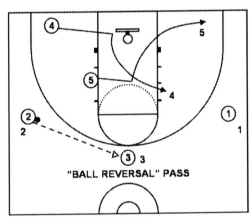

"BALL REVERSAL" PASS

Diagram 5.43

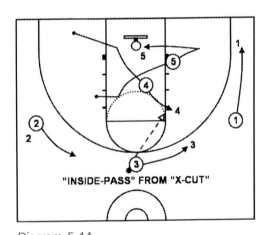

"INSIDE-PASS" FROM "X-CUT"

Diagram 5.44

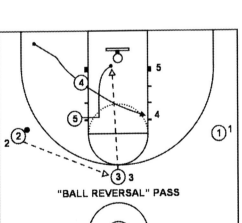

"BALL REVERSAL" PASS

Diagram 5.45

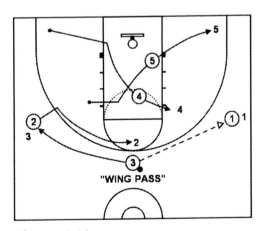

"WING PASS"

Diagram 5.46

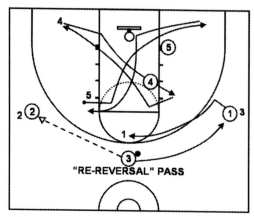

Diagram 5.47

To protect the interior of the zone defense, often times a defense will slough off extra defenders from the perimeter area to help their interior defenders. This movement of players will strengthen the interior of the zone defense but will weaken the perimeter. This weakness must be taken advantage of swiftly by making one (or two) skip passes from the ballside to the weakside (#3, #15).

Diagrams 5.48 and 5.49 illustrate the defense dropping perimeter defenders off to help prevent the ballside post (O5) and the short-corner (O4) from scoring inside. This change should help free up the weakside wing (O3). This weakness is attacked by the ballside wing (O2) recognizing the defensive congestion on the inside and not forcing the ball there. Instead, O2 skip-passes the ball cross-court to O3, who should have his feet and hands ready to catch the ball and quickly shoot (#13, #15).

A made three-point shot loosens up the congestion of a tightly packed-in defense like nothing else. The 3.5 players on the original ballside should anticipate the shot and look to overload the new weakside for offensive rebounds (Diagram 5.48) (#6).

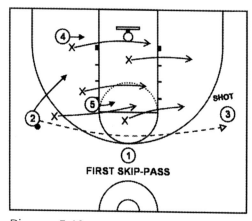

Diagram 5.48

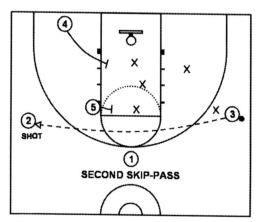

Diagram 5.49

Sometimes a zone defense will anticipate and aggressively react to the skip pass with an eager pursuit of the skip pass. This apparent strength of the defense can be transformed into a defensive weakness. When O3 receives the skip pass and reads the over-anxious defense swarming to the ball to deny the three-point shot, he simply skip passes the ball back from where it originally came. The over-pursuing defense must stop and react by then returning to the original ballside. In the heavy zone offense, the original short corner and ballside post can then pin-screen zone defenders who are chasing the ball from one side of the court to the other. This simple counter by the offense horizontally stretches the defense, providing a weakened defense both on the perimeter as well as in the interior of the zone defense. The second skip-pass ultimately discourages the opposition from hustling so much to close out on the initial skip-pass. The defense then gives the offense more opportunities after skip passes (Diagram 5.49) (#3, #15, #18).

Another counter move by the offense is to have the pass-receiver catch the pass and look for a three-point shot. If no shot is available, the receiver looks for a seal move to an inside post player (after the post player has pin-screened for the weakside perimeter player). This opportunity is often available after the defense has been weakened in the middle. The pin-screen followed by the seal move can only be executed after the second skip-pass in the heavy zone offense, since there was no pin-screen and seal move after the original skip pass (#15, #18, #24).

An option, which can be utilized with the heavy zone offense continuity, is a minor adjustment from the reversal pass rule (#9). Normally both inside players make their x-cuts when the ball is reversed. Instead of always making this cut, the two could make straight cuts. This move simply consists of the short-corner (O5) making a gap-cut along the baseline and eventually arriving at the same short-corner position on the opposite side of the floor. While this move is taking place, the ballside post (O4 in the diagram) makes a gap cut and crosses the lane to remain in his same post area, but on the opposite side (#22).

If the wing pass is made by the point (O2 in this illustration) to the opposite wing (O3), he still flare-exchanges with O1. The option has allowed the offense to attack the defense differently. If nothing develops after the ball reversal and the post-player's straight cuts, all five players are still in the heavy's spot-up positions, ready to continue the relentless attack on the opposition (Diagram 5.50) (#26).

Because of the basic three principles (different entries with one set; same entry out of different sets out of different entries; different sets) a coaching staff can, with a little imagination, use any entry in this book with any set and can change them at will. A coach can even use the perimeter entries with different post maneuvers using the set that best fits your personnel for the year. For example, a team can use the dribble gap technique, then pass to a wing and exchange, and combine these perimeter

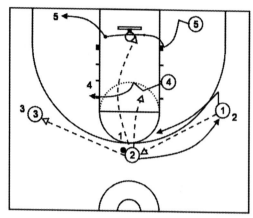

Diagram 5.50

maneuvers with a choice of the post cuts presented throughout this book: x-cuts, pin-screens, duck-ins, straight cuts, and so on.

A coaching staff can actually build its own zone offense using any entry with any perimeter cut and the post cuts. A team can start in one set and end in the spot-ups of one zone continuity offense, and by using various options, could end up in the spot-up locations of a different continuity. This versatility will give a team a zone offense that appears multiple when actually it is very simple and easy to teach.

Three more examples depicting different entries from different sets ending in the heavy continuity spot-up positions are you, me, and double. All three of these entries begin with the dribble gap technique.

The first entry is called *you* and is initiated by O1 gap dribbling between the two defensive wings on top and by passing the ball to either wing (#12). The even man (O4) takes the high road and makes a gap cut to the dotted circle before then chasing the wing pass and always going to the ballside post position, while the odd man (O5) takes the low road by cutting low to the basket before also chasing the wing pass and thus going to the new ballside short-corner (Diagrams 5.51 and 5.52). This entry attacks the defense's middle interior and the short-corner area (#3). O1 gap dribbles, passes the ball to either wing, and then exchanges with the wing player who did not receive the pass. All five players are now in the proper spot-up positions for the heavy zone offense continuity to be run for as long as needed (Diagrams 5.51 and 5.52) (#26).

The second entry is called *me* and is a mirror entry to the *you* entry/play. The only difference is that the two post players switch their initial cuts in the lane, but both still chase the ball on the wing pass and go to the ballside post and the ballside short corner respectively. Therefore, O5 takes the duck-in route and then settles in at the new ballside post area, while O4 steps towards the basket and looks for the lob pass from O1. If no lob pass is made, he now becomes the post player that goes to the new ballside short-corner area. The perimeter players have identical responsibilities as in the *you* entry, placing all five players again in the heavy zone offense continuity spot-ups (Diagrams 5.53 and 5.54).

Diagram 5.51

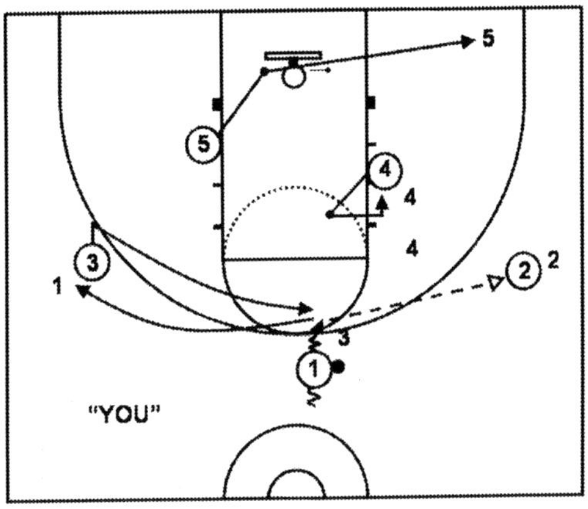

Diagram 5.52

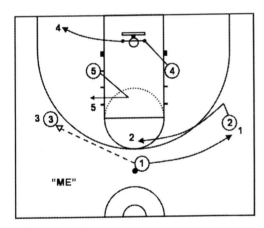

Diagram 5.53

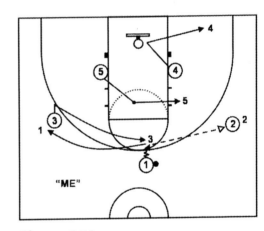

Diagram 5.54

The third entry also is initiated by O1 gap dribbling into the gap between the two wings, this time with both post players ducking in to the dotted circle, before both dropping back down to the original block positions. This entry is called *double* and attacks the interior middle of the defense, by overloading it with both post players ducking in before returning to their original low post position (#3). If the point guard doesn't hit either post player, he passes the ball to either wing (O2 in Diagram 5.55) and exchanges with the opposite wing (O3). The post player who ends up on the new weakside (O5) then curls around the new ballside post (O4) to the new ballside short corner. Now, all are again in the proper spot-up positions for the heavy zone offense continuity to continue (Diagram 5.55) (#26).

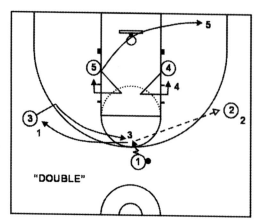

"DOUBLE"

Diagram 5.55

While these three examples of quick hitters begin from the split set and end in the heavy continuity spot-up positions, you can actually begin from any of the other sets (the 2-1-2, the 1-3-1, the 2-3, or the 2-1-2 off set), run these same three entries, and end in the heavy continuity offense (or end in any of the other continuities a coaching staff wishes).

These are but three examples of quick hitters from different sets into the heavy continuity offense. Coaches do not have to be limited to only these three entries or to starting from the split set. Any entry discussed in this book can be used to get from any alignment/set into any and all continuity offenses. The multiple zone offense is limited only by the coaching staff's imagination and creativity.

To further illustrate this point, let's look at three entries from the stack set and let each end in the heavy continuity spot-up positions. These three entries are called *read*, *double-cross*, and *middle*.

From these examples, a coach should see the beauty of the attacking zone defenses using the basic three principle: use different entries with only one set, use same entry with different sets, or use different entries with different sets. And the staff can make any of these entries conclude in the spot-up position of their choice. From that point, a team can run the continuity that goes with that spot-up position, or change to another continuity with different spot-up positions. All the entries with certain options in this book can be made to flow from one continuity to another continuity, giving a team a never-ending, non-repeating, multiple zone offense with very little extra to teach (#5, #26).

The Stack Alignment/Set

The stack set overloads the zone defense at the very beginning and often places the second post player (O5) behind the zone defense (#3, #4, #16). This alignment is the same alignment that can and is utilized before then flowing into the rotation continuity zone offense previously described. After any entry has been executed and no shot or turnover takes place, the stack set/alignment could have all five players in the heavy zone offense continuity spot-ups.

Several entries that can be run out of the stack set are described in the following and all end up in the heavy zone offense continuity offense's spot-up positions, which will allow this offense to continue its attack on the defense (#26). Most entries out of this alignment are initiated by O1 gap dribbling into the gap between the two wing defenders on the top of the zone (#12). These entries/plays will be shown when executed out of the stack set/alignment when the post players are stacked on the left side. Each entry could also be run when stacked on the right side. The first entry called *read* is initiated with the same gap dribble, while the even man (O4) takes the high road and ducks in to the dotted circle and the odd man (O5) takes the low road and cuts low. The two cuts these post players make are not always on specific tracks, but instead are wherever the gaps exist in the zone defense (#22). If the point guard doesn't hit either post player, he passes the ball to either wing and both post players *read* (hence the entry's name) the wing pass and follow it, as O4 goes to the ballside post area and O5 to the ballside short-corner area. This action could go towards either wing, but in this scenario, the first wing pass is made to O2. This action first attacks the defense's middle interior and then the defense's vulnerable short-corner area (#3). Diagram 5.56 shows the *read* entry with the point guard (O1) passing the ball to the wing (O2) on the right side. After the wing pass, O1 exchanges with the wing player who did not receive the pass (O3 in Diagram 5.56). Again, all five players are now in the proper spot-up positions for the heavy zone offense continuity to be run as long as necessary (#26).

The second entry out of the stacks set is called *double-cross*. This entry is simply the *read* entry/play, but with O4 and O5 exchanging cuts and reads on the wing pass. This play also is initiated by O1 gap dribbling into the gap between the two defensive wing-players on top as O4 and O5 are simply *double-crossing* the zone defense on their cuts into the lane. The odd man (O5) switches his cut and now takes the high road on his gap-cut as he ducks in to the dotted circle, while the even man (O4) exchanges with his teammate and now takes the low route (#12). The three perimeter players execute the entry the same as they do in the *read* entry. Both post players again follow the wing pass to the new ballside as O5 goes to the ballside post area and O4 goes to the ballside short-corner area, thus again placing all five players in the proper spot-up positions of the heavy zone offense continuity (Diagram 5.57).

The third entry out of the stacks set, titled *middle*, initially appears the same as the first two entries, which should cause confusion and doubt to the defense. The post player on top of the stack (O4) reads the zone to determine what defender covers the middle of the zone and then steps into the lane to screen the designated defender. Afterwards, he settles in and posts up on the same block where he started. The low man on the stack (O5) cuts off of his teammate's (O4) interior screen into the heart of the zone defense, looking for the ball from the point guard (O1) (#18). If O5 doesn't receive the ball, he continues across the lane to the vacant block position. Both players post up for a full two counts, looking to catch the ball from the point. If the point guard doesn't hit either post player, he makes a wing pass to either wing or then makes a flare exchange with the opposite wing. With the ball at one particular wing, a ballside post can then be declared (O4 in Diagram 5.58) and he then steps out of the post into the new ballside short corner. The new weakside post (O5 in Diagram 5.59) makes a gap cut through the lane before settling in at the new ballside post area (#12). Diagrams 5.58 and 5.59 illustrate the *middle* entry/play run to the left side, but this entry can be also run to the right side.

Other entries out of this alignment can be created for specific player's strengths to be utilized and taken advantage of (#6). Also, other alignments/sets could be devised with its own family of entries/plays.

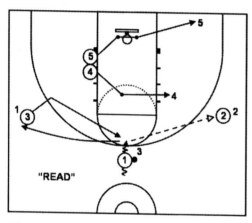

Diagram 5.56

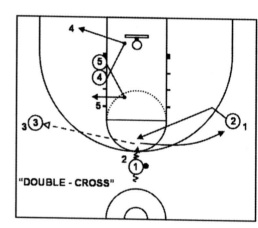

Diagram 5.57

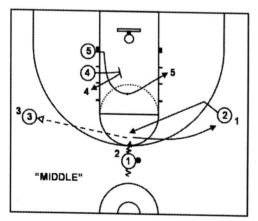

Diagram 5.58

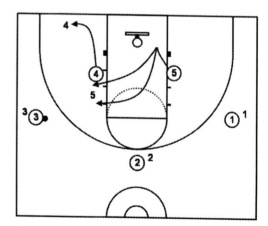

Diagram 5.59

Breakdown Drills for the
Heavy Zone Continuity Offense

Besides using the breakdown drill presented earlier in this chapter, you should add two specific drills just for the heavy zone continuity. On the right side of the court, in Diagram 5.60, the post players are learning the movements and developing the timing of the two post players when a pass is made into the short corner from the ballside wing. On the left side of the court, the two post players are learning the movements and developing the timing when the pass is made to the side post from the ballside wing.

Diagram 5.61 displays the basic inside movement of the heavy zone continuity. This exercise is a two-ball drill. The first ball starts in the possession of the short corner. The short corner passes out to the ballside wing who immediately passes to the new point guard (weakside wing breaks to the point position). The two posts make their x-cuts (for more on x-cut maneuvers, see Chapter 8) as the ball is being reversed. The point guard immediately passes inside to the player cutting from the short corner into the high post for his maneuver and shot. Meanwhile, the second ball is used to pass to the player cutting from the side post to the low post.

This drill could be continued by not passing the second ball to the player cutting from the side post until he reaches the short corner. So, the original short corner cutter (now at the high post) would be compelled to break down to the low post (ballside) for a pass and a maneuver and shot.

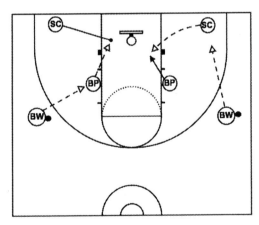

Diagram 5.60

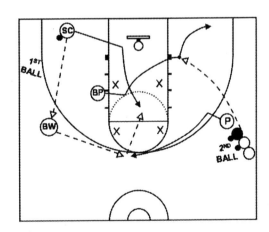

Diagram 5.61

Conclusion

The heavy and rotation continuities are fundamentally sound offenses that apply many basic philosophies and concepts. Many of these concepts can capitalize on different weaknesses of the zone defense (#3). Every phase of the game is clearly laid out as to player assignments to make the offense a carefully planned out zone offense, efficient in every part of the game (#5). The offensive rebounding phase (#8), the defensive transition phase (#7), and the offensive transition phase (#1), as well as the actual entries/plays out of the various alignments/sets (#2, #4), should all be carefully planned out, taught and coached, and thoroughly practiced repeatedly for the offense to be completely efficient.

Having the flexibility of being able to use different alignments/sets allows this offense to attack various types of zone defenses that have even or odd fronts (e.g., 2-1-2 zones, 2-3 zones, 1-2-2 zones, 1-3-1 zones, and 1-1-3 zones). Once the ball is in the deep corner, most zones are pretty much the same in placement of their defensive personnel. With the rotation zone offense, the offense will have the opportunity of being able to use different alignments/sets, which gives the offense an important advantage of being able to use different entries/plays against the opposition's defense. This approach makes it extremely difficult for the opposition to scout, prepare for, and ultimately to defend against the rotation zone offense. Each entry can be designed to take advantage of individual player's specific offensive strengths and/or capitalize on individual opponent's weaknesses or that particular zone defense's weaknesses.

Yet, with the flexibility and multiple options that the rotation zone offense possesses, it still remains a simple offense for players to be able to perform. With each position being a specialized position, each position player clearly knows his responsibilities and assignments and each position player can hone his offensive skills and be able to perform them at a high degree of efficiency. With a coaching staff developing and utilizing breakdown drills for each position, players can have a great advantage in improving individual play as well as continually learning that specific position's responsibilities and assignments. This zone offense continually improves as a whole as each individual player improves in his knowledge and understanding of the offense, as well as the specific offensive skills that are required for it to be successful. The offense becomes more and more efficient with its use both in practice and in games.

6

The Triple-Post Zone Continuity Offense

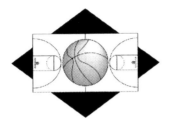

Introduction to the Triple-Post Offense

The triple-post zone offense can attack both on the perimeter and in the interior of various zone defenses. For the triple-post zone offense to be successful, the offense needs all five of the offensive players to be in the proper offensive locations on the floor (called spot-up positions) and for all players to follow the specific rules that apply for each type of pass that can be made in this offense. Multiple options (that help prevent the offense from being predictable and scoutable by opposing teams) are important supplements of this offense and can easily be added, but are not necessary (#2). The offense not only attacks the zone defense's weaknesses, but also counters the zone defense's strengths, initially with particular entries or certain counter-options within the actual continuity rules of the offense (#3).

A team using this zone offense can have, within its offensive scheme, multiple secondary fast breaks, with all being able to flow directly into the zone offense continuity (#1). If the secondary fast break does not produce transition points, each secondary break utilized must end up in the same five offensive spot-ups the zone offense continuity possesses.

Because of the flexibility this continuity offense has, the offense is able to have entries/plays that flow into the continuity offense—assuming the entry/play does not produce a score. These entries can take advantage of individual offensive player's specific strengths (#6). If an offensive team is aware of specific individual weaknesses of the opposition, multiple entries can allow the offensive team to use particular entries to take advantage of those known weaknesses of individual zone defenders (#6).

All entries in this chapter can be run out of the split or the stack sets discussed in previous chapters. Those alignments can easily be added or deleted from the offensive package (#2, #4, #6). Hence, all three of the basic attack principles are available: same entry, different sets; different entries, different sets; and different entries, same sets.

If scores do not result in these quick-hitters, the five players will culminate in the spot-ups and the offensive attack can continue indefinitely. This alignment keeps the zone offense in a continuous attack mode, thus preventing the opposition's defense from recovering or relaxing (#26).

The five spot-up locations of this zone offense allow for maximum offensive rebounding effectiveness. Even if the plays or the actual continuity gives the offensive team great shot selection and the offensive team shoots at a 50 percent field goal percentage, the other 50 percent of the field goal attempts will still be missed (#8).

As important as offensive rebounding is, the triple-post zone offense also has specific defensive transition responsibilities for every offensive player. These responsibilities remove all confusion for any of the offensive players regarding their offensive rebounding, as well as transition assignments (#7).

The triple-post zone offense has specific rules to flatten out the zone defense on one side of the floor and overload that same side of the floor with four players (#4, #17). The offense wants to then quickly reverse the ball and try to beat the defense to perimeter shooting locations on the opposite side of the floor. While the offense attacks the defense on the perimeter in this manner, it still attacks the opposition on the interior, by having players attack the zone from behind and by having post players making various gap cuts into the heart of the zone defense (#16, #22, #24).

This attack with ball reversal makes the zone a balanced offense by being a threat both on the perimeter as well as the interior. Post players near the free-throw line can become passers to potential scorers on the perimeter, while perimeter players can also become passers to scorers in either the high post or the low-post areas (#6, #10, #13, #14, #21).

The triple-post zone offense stretches the zone defense both vertically as well as horizontally, with a player in the deep ballside corner, the ballside wing, the weakside wing, the ballside low-post, and also the ballside high-post areas. This approach weakens the opposition's defense, as well as providing safe passing lanes for the ball to be passed inside and on the perimeter to the opposite side of the court (#11).

Placement of Personnel

Using the standard numbering system, O1 should be the point guard, O2 should be the big guard, O3 is the small forward, O4 is the power forward, and O5 is the center. O1 should be the best ball handler and interior passer, but all perimeter players should be good at passing and using the specific types of dribbles used in zone offenses. It is important that all three perimeter players know the various types of zone dribbles, passes, and how to utilize all of them effectively at the appropriate times (#12).

It is also extremely important that all three of the perimeter players (O1, O2, and O3) be outstanding perimeter shooters, particularly off of the pass. Stretching the defense both vertically and horizontally and being able to probe the inside of the zone defense are vital goals of the triple-post continuity.

The two post players should be the best rebounders and they are assigned full-time offensive rebounding assignments, with the best rebounder of the three perimeter players added to that group. The best defender of the two remaining perimeter players is assigned the sole responsibility of getting back on defense, while the remaining perimeter player is assigned a responsibility that entails both rebounding and getting back on defense. That player is the only player that has two responsibilities: part rebounder and part defensive safety (#9).

As the name suggests, the triple-post zone offense requires three post players (most likely O5, O4, and O3). O3 is the player who is the combination of a perimeter player as well as a post player. These three post players must be able to read the defense—particularly the interior defense. These three players must be able to work well together and be able to read each other's interior cuts, as there will be gap cuts made by the two post players, as well as the perimeter player who started in the ballside deep corner.

Spot-up Locations and Descriptions

The spot-ups for the triple-post zone offense continuity are somewhat different than the spot-ups of many other zone offenses. The basic spot-up positions have half of the court as the ballside, with the opposite side being called the weakside or the offside. The spot-ups are set up in an even front alignment, having a ballside wing, a weakside wing, a ballside low post, a ballside high post, and a ballside baseline corner. The ballside wing and a weakside wing are located just above the (imaginary) free-throw line extended, just outside the three-point line on both sides of the court. These spots can be called the wide elbow areas. The ballside low-post position is always on the first notch above the low-post block on the ballside. The ballside high-post position is always at the intersection of the free-throw lane line and the actual free-throw line on the ballside, which is called the tight elbow area. The baseline corner position is a step off the baseline and midway between the block and the sideline, and always on the ballside.

The offense can be run from either the left side or the right side of the court. Diagram 6.1 shows the spot-up locations if the ball is on the left side, while Diagram 6.2 shows the same spot-ups when the ball is on the right side (Diagrams 6.1 and 6.2). The entries and options will only be shown from the right side of the court. They are the same on the left side.

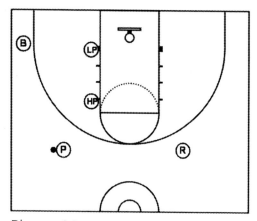

Diagram 6.1   Diagram 6.2

The Triple-Post Continuity

Diagram 6.3 displays the basic continuity. O1 freeze dribbles and passes to O2 (#12). As this pass occurs, O5 cuts to the corner. O3 and O4 run the x-cut, described later in this chapter. These post cuts can occur either when O2 has the ball or when O5 has received the down pass from O2 (#21, #22, #23, #24, #25). After the ball has been passed to O5, O1 and O2 exchange spot-up positions. The ball has been reversed from the left side of the floor to the right side (#17).

Diagram 6.4 shows the continuity from the left side of the floor. O1 executes the freeze dribble and passes to O2 (#12). O4 cuts to the corner. O3 and O5 run the x-cut (#21, #22, #23, #24, #25). When the ball is passed from O2 to O4, O1 and O2 exchange spot-up positions. The continuity now has been run completely (#26).

Now let's explain the stationary entries before going into some special options. In Diagram 6.5, you can see the overload on the right side of the floor. This method is one of the basic ways of attacking any zone defense—the overload. O1 has several options. He can pass to the corner. He can pass to the corner (A in the diagram). O3

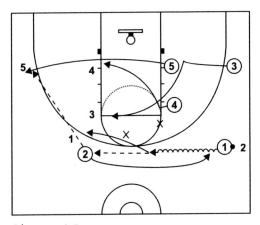

Diagram 6.3

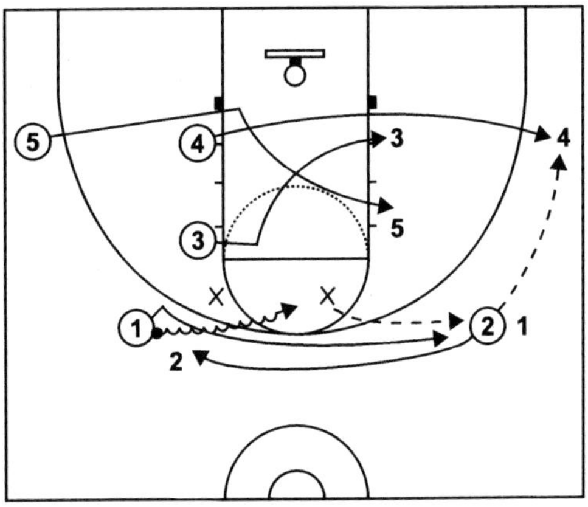

Diagram 6.4

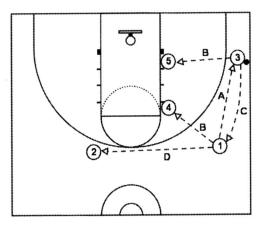

Diagram 6.5

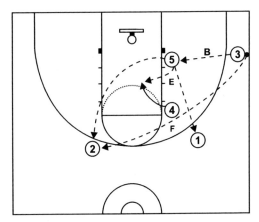

Diagram 6.6

can shoot or pass inside to O5 (B in the diagram), who should have sealed his defender on the upper side (#23, #24, #25). O5 can shoot or can look to pass to the cutting O4 (E in Diagram 6.6) (#20). Or, O5 can pass to the perimeter players who should have moved to open spot-up positions on the perimeter (#21).

Diagram 6.7 exhibits the pass from O1 to O4. O4 should immediately turn to see if O5 has managed to get position on his defender (#20). O5 has a great advantage on his defender regardless of how the defender wishes to play. If O5's defender fronts O5, the lob pass is available. If O5's defender plays below or on either side, O5 should be able to seal him for a pass from O4 (#24, #25).

Another option is shown in Diagram 6.8. O3 skip passes to O2 (#15). O2 now has the option of passing to either O4 or O5 as the post players cut to the gaps (#22). Or, O5 can cut to the corner while O4 and O3 run the x-cut of the continuity.

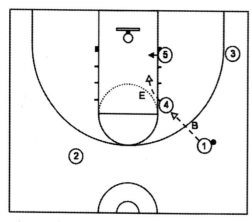

Diagram 6.7

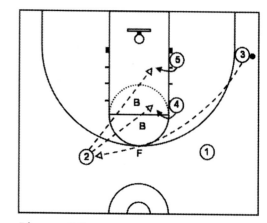

Diagram 6.8

Diagram 6.9 is a continuation of Diagram 6.8. As the defense recovers to defend the quick reversal by the skip pass, O2 merely skip passes back to O3. Meanwhile, O5 and O4 have set pin-screens on the defenders to keep them from covering the three-point shot of O3 (#15, #18). The combination of the two skip passes is almost impossible to cover. If the defense does not react to the first skip pass (Diagram 6.8), they cannot defend the perimeter shot by O2 or the inside play of O4 and O5. Defenders must get on the goal side of the post players to prevent the inside pass. However, if they do react to the first skip pass, the second skip pass cannot be defended (Diagram 6.9). By reacting to defend the first skip pass, the defenders are on the inside of the post players, and therefore are easily screened from getting back out to cover O3.

Let's now consider the dribble techniques of the continuity. Diagram 6.10 shows the gap dribble technique. O1 dribbles in the gap of the defenders while the triple-

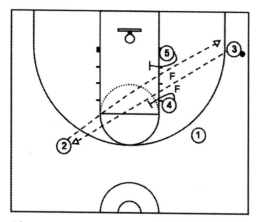

Diagram 6.9

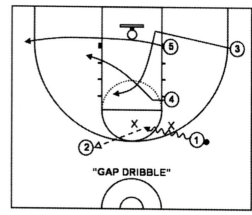

Diagram 6.10

post players run the continuity. O2 positions himself for a possible pass and a quick score. O1 has the option of passing to O2, O3 (skip pass), O4, or O5 (inside pass). If a defender covers O2, then O3 must be open or the zone will really be distorted (#4, #12, #15).

P begins the next dribbling techniques of the continuity using the freeze dribble. R finds the open spot in the perimeter while the post players run the options of the triple-post continuity. The defense is distorted again if the defense tries to prevent R from getting his shot. P has options available to pass to R, to B, to HP, or to LP (#4, #12, #15).

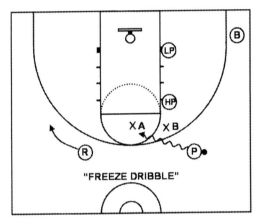

Diagram 6.11

Offensive Rebounding and Transition Responsibilities

One method to strongly emphasize to the three potentially best offensive rebounders of the triple-post zone offense is to assign them the unique name of fullback. Doing so should help remind them that their only responsibility is to rebound offensively out of the zone offense. The three fullbacks should form a triangular cup around the basket two to three feet from the basket, with the main points of emphasis to not get drawn in too far under the basket and to snatch the offensive rebound with two hands and quickly power the ball up. If the ball cannot be secured with two hands, sometimes a back tip out to the halfback might be the next best way of obtaining an offensive rebound. When offensive players see that the defense has rebounded the basketball, the two biggest fullbacks should then run lanes as if they were running their own offensive fast break. This hustle may lead the two post players to possible intercepted passes by the opposition, but at the minimum, it gets them back to help defend their own basket with their teammates. In the triple-post zone offense, the designated fullbacks would most likely be the three post players: O3, O4, and O5.

The fourth best rebounder is the zone offense's half-rebounder and half-defensive safety—otherwise known as the halfback. His responsibility is half offensive rebounding and half getting back on defensive transition. The halfback should quickly get to the weakside elbow area opposite of where the shot was taken. When he also sees that the missed shot is defensively rebounded by the opposition, only then should he get out and run his normal offensive fast break lane and sprint to the other end of the floor as quickly as possible. The halfback also might accidentally cause the opposition to commit turnovers, or at least congest their offensive fast break lanes, slowing them down. In the triple-post zone offense, the designated halfback would most likely be the rebounder or the 2 man.

The smallest defender has absolutely no rebounding responsibilities. He strictly is to get back on defense and to prevent the opponents from getting easy scores from their offensive fast breaks. He is called the tailback, for his one and only job is to get his tail back on defense (Diagram 6.12) (#7, #8).

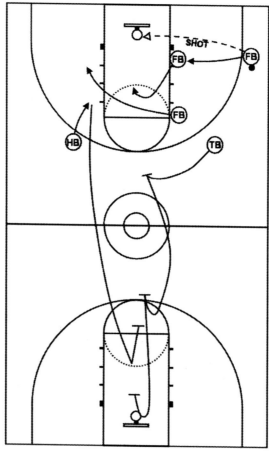

Diagram 6.12

Primary Fast Break into the Secondary Fast Break into the Zone Continuity Offense

Any primary fast breaks and any full-court press offenses chosen must have a free-flowing and easy blend into the secondary fast break. This approach makes every one of the fast break opportunities a scoring weapon, but also a conduit immediately into the continuity zone offense (#1).

The opposition is allowed no time to rest or to reassemble their zone defense properly, which may cause the defense to be greatly weakened—giving the offense still another advantage over the opposition. Even though many different secondary fast breaks could be utilized, Diagrams 6.13 and 6.14 show just one secondary fast break that is an easy fit into the triple-post zone offense.

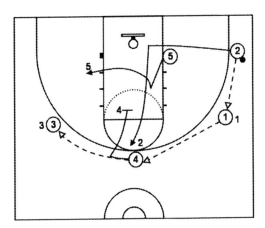

Diagram 6.13   Diagram 6.14

Diagram 6.13 exhibits one of the options of the secondary break presented in Chapter 2 (#1). The ball has been reversed from O2 to O1 to O4 to O3 (or a skip pass could have been used (#10, #15, #17). O3 uses the pull dribble to adjust into the triple-post continuity spot-ups (#12). This move puts all five offensive personnel in the spot-ups of the triple-post continuity, with O3 in the corner, O5 at low post, O4 at high post, and with the exchange between O1 and O2, O1 will be the left guard and O2 the right guard. Now all the options previously present are available for the triple-post continuity: the dribble techniques and the passing techniques. However, more importantly, the attack has flowed smoothly from fast break to secondary break to continuity. Also, the three fundamental principles of attack against zones are all available: different entries, same set; same entries, different sets; different entries, different sets.

Three plays out of the split set/alignment, in which all easily flow into the spot-ups of the triple-post continuity offense, are shown in Diagrams 6.15 through 6.17. These three plays are named *north* (6.15), *south* (6.16), and *west* (6.17) respectively. The first two dictate which post player (O4) in the *north* entry and (O5) in the south entry make the strong duck-in cut to the dotted circle in the middle of the lane. The opposite post player steps towards the basket. If neither post player receives the inside pass after O1 makes the penetrating gap dribble and passes the ball to either wing, post players then go straight across the lane to post up on the newly declared ballside post areas. If the wing that receives the wing pass (O2 in Diagram 6.15 and O3 in Diagram 6.16) cannot shoot quickly or pass the ball inside to either post player, he pull dribbles down to the deep corner. This move also forces O1 over to the wing area. If the wing still cannot make the inside pass, the entry/play is over with all personnel now in the spot-ups of the triple-post continuity offense (Diagram 6.15 and 6.16).

The third entry, called *west*, dictates that only O3 cuts behind the post players through the lane and on to the deep corner on the opposite side of the court (#16, #17, #22). On O1's gap dribble, O5 ducks-in as he does in the *south* entry/play (#12, #22). O4 remains on his original low-post area to pin-screen for O3 (#18). If O1 does not hit O5 on the duck-in or hit O3 for a lob pass, he must hit O2 at the wing. O2 has the option of quickly shooting off of the pass, passing down to O3 in the deep corner, passing to O4 on the new ballside block, or passing to O5 who flashed to the new ballside high post. If none of these scoring options are fruitful, the *west* play is over. It has succeeded in at least placing personnel in the triple-post continuity offense spot-ups. When the ball is ultimately reversed from O1 to O2 now on the weakside, O3, O4, and O5 makes the x-cuts to end up in the triple-post continuity offense spot-ups on the opposite side of the court (#17, #22).

Another offensive alignment/set that can be utilized in a half-court setting is a set called stacks. O1 is the point guard, O2 is at the right wing, and O3 is at the left wing. O5 aligns on the first notch above the block, with O4 adjacent and above O5. O5 and O4 could stack together on the left side (Diagram 6.18) or on the right side (Diagram 6.19) (#4).

For discussion's sake, the three entries/plays out of the stacks set/alignment are all shown out of the stacks-right set/alignment. These three entries are very similar to the three entries mentioned previously out of the split set. The cuts and dribbling techniques are very similar. What is identical to the split set entries are that if these three entries do not produce immediate points, it does reposition all players into the proper spot-ups for the triple-post continuity to immediately begin at the entry's conclusion.

The *sam* entry (strongside) and the *will* entry (weakside) dictate which wing O1 passes to after making the same gap dribble. The post players make the same cuts in all three entries—O4 ducks in to the dotted circle, waits, and flashes to the new ballside high post. O5 steps behind the defense, towards the basket, and looks for a lob pass from O1. He then steps to the new ballside low post once the ballside has been declared with O1's wing pass. The new ballside wing (O2 in Diagram 6.20 and O3 in

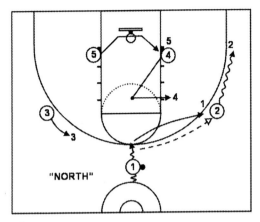

Diagram 6.15

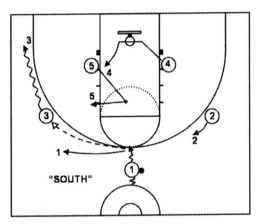

Diagram 6.16

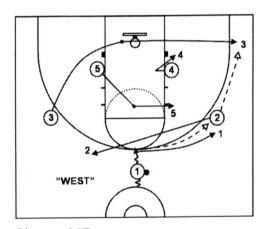

Diagram 6.17

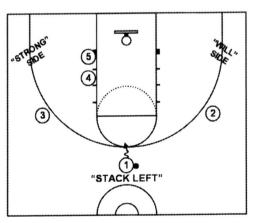

Diagram 6.18

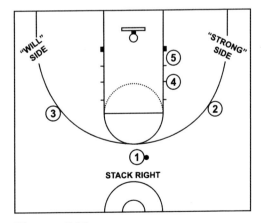

Diagram 6.19

Diagram 6.21) looks to hit either flashing post players and then dribbles down to the deep corner to improve the passing angles inside, as well as to stretch and flatten the defense (#17). O1 rotates over to complete the filling of all five spot-up positions for the continuity offense to begin and continue the perpetual attack on the defense.

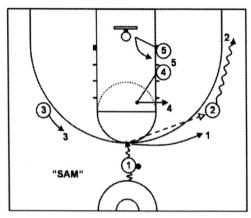

Diagram 6.20

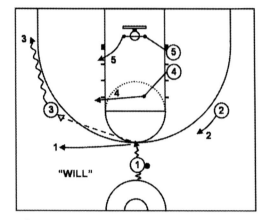

Diagram 6.21

Diagram 6.22 illustrates the third entry out of the stacks set/alignment that will also position all personnel into the spot-ups of the triple-post continuity offense. This *mike* entry is very similar to the *west* entry executed out of the split set/alignment. O3 cuts behind the zone, through the lane and on to the opposite deep corner as O1 makes his gap dribble (#12, #16). O1 must look inside to O4 on his same duck-in cut or make the perimeter wing pass only to O2. O2 looks for his quick shot off of the pass, an inside pass to O4 at the high post, an inside pass to O5 on the low post, or to the deep corner to O3 (#13). Again, offensive personnel are in the proper spot-ups so that the continuity offense can immediately pick up as the play concludes.

Regardless of what alignment/set is used to start the offense (split set and stack sets are discussed), if the entry/play does not produce immediate points scored, then unique spot-up positions for just this zone continuity offense are always filled with the correct offensive players. When the entry is concluded, the positioning of the players allows the continuity offense to immediately begin with no delay. Diagram 6.23 illustrates the cuts and movement of the triple-post continuity offense when the ball is reversed. The rotation of the original low-post player (O4) then becomes the next ballside corner on the opposite side. The current ballside corner (O3) becomes the next ballside high-post player, while the current high-post player (O5) becomes the next low-post player. After the passes made to the deep corner, the two perimeter wings switch locations so that O1 always ends up as the ballside wing and O2 is always the weakside wing (Diagram 6.23). The offense can continue its attack for an indefinite period of time, always on the attack (#26).

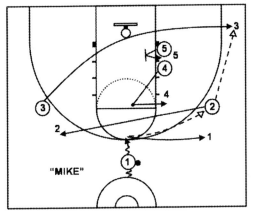
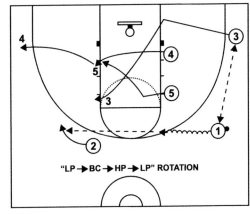

Diagram 6.22   Diagram 6.23

Breakdown Drills for the Zone Offense

A creative coaching staff can (and should) design their own drills to strengthen the offensive fundamentals of their players that are required to make their particular offense more effective. Drills should be organized so that whatever skills and techniques are being practiced will be practiced in the same locations they would be performed in a game, and only by those individuals that will perform them in games.

Passing drills for specific players in certain positions should be pass-receiving drills for other players in the same drills. Where players will most likely shoot the ball during games are the locations where players should practice the various shooting drills that are used. Most of the shooting drills are set up in the 55-second shooting/offensive drill format, where one player in the drill is called the rebounder, one is called the passer, and one called the shooter (remember this setup is part of the standard 55-second structure in most of the shooting drills). When involving only two shooters, use the rebounder to simulate the passing, which occurs within the continuity.

Breakdown shooting and passing drills are given in Chapter 7 for all the continuities. In this section, we will also offer shooting and passing drills, as well as the movements that will teach, re-teach, and teach again the triple-post continuity.

Diagram 6.24 shows a skip passing drill along with shooting. P skip passes to S and S can shoot or skip pass back to P (#10, #11, #13, #14, #15). A rebounder, R, should be added to work on the outlet pass.

Diagram 6.25 displays the initial wing entry pass, which begins the triple-post continuity. Again, a rebounder is shown in the drill to work on the outlet pass (#11, #13, #14).

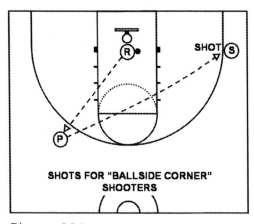

Diagram 6.24

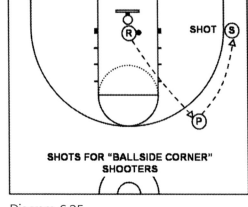

Diagram 6.25

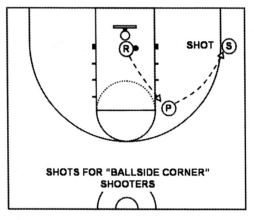

Diagram 6.26

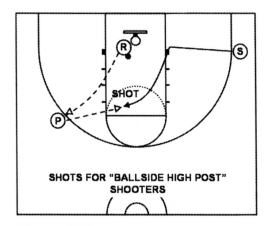

Diagram 6.27

Diagram 6.26 illustrates the high post to corner pass or the corner to high-post pass. This pass is frequently available in the triple-post continuity (#13, #14, #21, #22, #23, #24, #25).

The first cutting drill we will present is shown in Diagram 6.27. P receives the outlet pass from R, which simulates a pass from the opposite guard or a skip pass from the opposite corner (#15, #16, #20). S moves from the corner into the baseline part of the x-cut of the triple-post continuity for the shot. R rebounds and continues the drill with another outlet pass to P (#20, #21, #22, #23, #24, #25).

Diagram 6.28 shows the high post part of the x-cut (#20, #21, #22, #23, #24, #25). P passes to S on the high-post cut.

Diagrams 6.29 and 6.30 display both angles of passing into the low post (#20, #21, #22, #23, #24, #25). If the low post does not have the shot, P finds the gap around the perimeter (#21). If you have forgotten what the concepts are, go back to

Chapter 1 and review (in this instance, #21, #22, #23, #24, #25) and you will see how to use all these concepts in this drill. It expands this drill as well as all the others drills we have offered. A good way to study the drill is to read the concepts (the # inside the parentheses) and you will see all the aspects of the drill.

Diagram 6.31 simulates the gap or the freeze dribble into a shot around the perimeter. P uses the freeze dribble while S repositions himself for the shot (#10, #12, #13, #14).

Diagram 6.32 demonstrates the high post looking inside then passing opposite part of the triple-post continuity (#21, #22, #23, #24, #25).

Diagram 6.33 simulates the outside member of the three post players breaking behind the defense, using a screen by the low post and receiving the down pass (#10, #13, #14, #16, #17, #18, #20, #21, #22, #23, #24, #25).

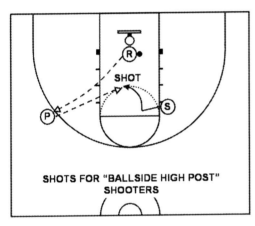

Diagram 6.28

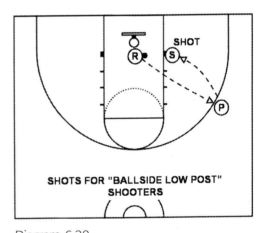

Diagram 6.29

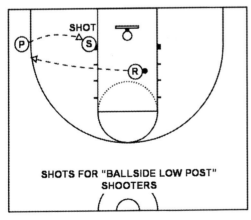

Diagram 6.30

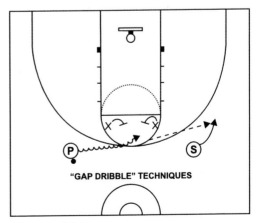

Diagram 6.31

The gap cuts of the three post players, as well as the x-cuts of the triple-post continuity, are drills in Diagram 6.34. You can even use three passers (shown in Diagram 6.28), so all three players will be receiving a pass and shooting on each cut (#20, #21, #22, #23, #24, #25). S, in Diagram 6.34, will receive simulated passes from the post players who pretend they are not open and must exercise Concept #20.

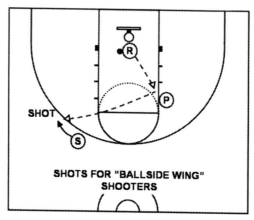

Diagram 6.32

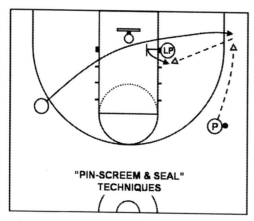

Diagram 6.33

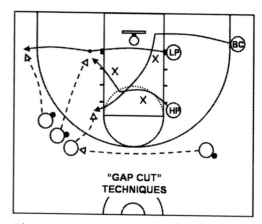

Diagram 6.34

Conclusion

The triple-post zone offense is an attacking type offense that utilizes and applies many sound philosophies, concepts, and theories. Many of these concepts can capitalize on the different weaknesses of the zone defense. Individual players' offensive responsibilities and assignments are clearly defined, making the offense a carefully planned out offense that allows players to be efficient in every part of the zone attack.

Being able to use different alignments allows this triple-post zone offense to attack various types of zone defenses that have either even or odd fronts (i.e., 2-1-2 zones, 2-3 zones, 1-2-2 zones, 1-3-1 zones, and 1-1-3 zones). Utilizing the triple-post zone offense gives a team the opportunity of being able to initiate the offense by using different sets, as well as various entries, before getting into the movements of the actual continuity.

Being able to implement different sets and entries gives an offensive team three distinct advantages. Each entry can be designed to take advantage of individual player's specific offensive strengths, capitalize on individual opponent's weaknesses, or that particular zone defense's weaknesses, as well as becoming less predictable.

Still, the triple-post zone offense remains a simple offense for offensive players to comprehend and understand, as well as to be able to perform. With each position being a specialized position, each position player clearly can learn and practice his responsibilities and assignments and can specialize his offensive skills to perform them at high degrees of efficiency. Developing and utilizing breakdown drills for each position gives each player an opportunity in improving his individual skills and an opportunity of a better understanding and comprehension of that position's responsibilities and assignments. The offense becomes more and more efficient with its use in practice and in games.

It is easy to see the complete philosophy at work. First is the fast break and the secondary break. Then the players are in spot-up positions to begin the continuity of your choice. You can allow the players to just stay stationary and use all the entries of the stationary positions. Specific entries can be called and then the entire continuity can be run. A change from one continuity to another in mid-possession is even possible. The three basic principles of the set offenses are at a coach's command: same set, different entries; different sets, different entries; and different sets, same entries.

7

Breakdown Drills

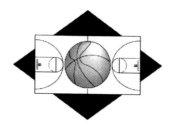

Zone offenses should be taught with a whole-part-whole teaching method. For example, Chapter 3, the baseline zone offense, should be taught and then broken down into its parts. Then the drills in this chapter should be used throughout the season to re-teach the parts of the zone offense, as well as the fundamentals needed to make the zone offense successful. Before offering the drills, a few hints are given on how to execute the drills properly.

- Have an organized practice plan—a coach's version of a lesson plan. Plan your work and work your plan. Don't vary too much from your plan, but be sure that some flexibility is included so that you are not completely bound by it. Use it as a guideline to accomplish everything that can be accomplished.

- Make sure the time limits of all drills are short enough that players do not get bored. A coach can plan to run a drill for four or five minutes, three different times in a practice, versus one, 15-minute drill setting, with players losing interest.

- Make sure that players are not just standing at the end of lines during drills. Create drills in which everyone is constantly involved, not just three or four players at a time.

- Make sure that all breakdown drills have gradually progressing levels of difficulty as players improve. This stipulation allows the positive reinforcement that players need as they initially learn and develop skills and techniques. It also keeps the players focused as they improve their skills.

- Set realistic performance goals for your players in the various practice drills, with the goals having a realistic similarity to the tough competition of games.

- Keep statistics on the players' performances in practice. Reward the winners in small ways and give small penalties for the losing individuals or teams.

- Demand from your players and assistant coaches a quick transition from one drill to the next. Don't let anyone waste time in the rotation between drills. Create a sense of urgency, which can be a great motivator for all players.

- Involve your assistant coaches in the practice planning and the actual teaching on the court. Effectively prepare the assistant coaches—and then let them teach.

- Make sure that the more sophisticated drills are game-realistic. In other words, these higher-level drills always must be performed at game speed and feature some form of pressure and competition. These drills should have winners and losers—with awards and (minimal) penalties.

- If you want your players to be enthusiastic and energetic, you must not only be enthusiastic and energetic yourself, but you must be the *most* enthusiastic and energetic person in the gym. Be an example to your players and coaching staff. As head coach, you must be the leader and set an example for all to follow. Let the players feed off your energy and enthusiasm.

- Don't accept anything but excellence from yourself, your staff, or your players. Players and assistant coaches will improve only if they are self-motivated or if they are pushed by others. Most players need to be motivated by the coaching staff.

- Have a keen eye for detail and expect the same from your players on every technique that is being taught and practiced. Include points of emphasis and coaching points in your practice plan with your assistant coaches and with your players.

- Be positive when correcting players and be critical in a positive way. Be demanding when it comes to your players' attention and physical effort. Don't accept anything below that high level that you constantly emphasize. Praise the team and the strong efforts of individual players. Let players know that you are well aware of the extraordinary hustle and effort of particular players. Doing so can reward those players and also motivate (in a subtle way) the players that could be putting forth a little more effort. Sometimes, though, certain players must be informed in a somewhat less subtle manner that their efforts need to be increased.

- Teach the rules of the game to your players. A team cannot succeed unless players follow the rules.

- Make your practices more demanding and tougher (both physically and mentally) than the games will demand.

- Establish your drills so that your players must concentrate as they perform them. Doing so will prepare players to focus more effectively in their games.

- Make sure you can combine drills so that there are frequent opportunities to work on the offense-to-defense transition, as well as the defense-to-offense transition. Organize and format many of your drills so that there will be a variety of competition (individual, small group, and team competition). Have a winner and a loser in the majority of the competitive drills, with the losers having some form of light penalty—possibly short sprints, push-ups, or sit-ups.

Offensive Drills and Fundamentals

In preparing your team to become more proficient in zone offenses, many drills could (and should) be utilized in that zone offense as education and preparation. Offensive fundamentals must be practiced with a great deal of effort, concentration, detail, and intensity—and with numerous repetitions exerted by the players as well as the coaching staff. This chapter includes various types of shooting drills that can be used to not only work on those shooting fundamentals, but also to maintain the high level of intensity and focus that is a requirement of all players for the drills to be successful.

The two transition drills that are described later in the chapter are extremely important for a zone offense to be successful. Even though zone offenses are primarily thought of in a half-court offense mindset, transitions between offense and defense are of the utmost importance. Both types of transitions—offense-to-defense and defense-to-offense—are an integral part of the foundation of any zone offense.

The routine outlined in Diagram 7.1 is designed for two 12-man teams and simultaneously works on stretching to prepare for practice and many of the game's fundamentals. The routine allows for short but concentrated time periods, covering a wide range of fundamentals necessary to build truly sound basketball players. It also sets the tone for an upbeat practice, forcing every player to concentrate on his individual and group responsibilities. This routine allows no room for boredom and standing around, as many activities last only 30-seconds to one minute. Only a couple of drills last more than one minute and those last only two to three minutes. The constant transition from one activity to another causes a great deal of attentiveness and concentration from every player. The first week of implementation of this routine can appear to be utter chaos, but in just a short period of time, the activity becomes organized stations. Twenty-four players can be involved at the same time in this routine in a gymnasium that has two main baskets and four supplemental side-court baskets. Each player needs to have his own basketball, and at least two energetic and mobile coaches should be observing, correcting, motivating, encouraging, coaching, and teaching all players involved. Each player will be part of a two-man group, a three-man group, and a six-man group. The players in these groups can be set and reset each day for variety and competition balance. Refer again to Diagram 7.1. The A represents the starter at a position and the B represents the second string player at the same position.

For example, 1A is the starting point guard (1), and 1B represents the second-string point guard (1). The 11 and 12 are the eleventh and twelfth players on the squad. This routine could be implemented in a summer camp format, in pre-season and/or post-season workouts, in physical educations classes, or at the beginning of in-season practices. It could be utilized before every practice or just specific practices as chosen by the coaching staff.

The entire gymnasium is broken down so that it may be utilized to its maximum efficiency. Each minute is valuable and keeping the transition between activities to a minimum is very important to obtain maximum utilization of time. The full-court diagram illustrates the general area for each of the areas/locations for the different

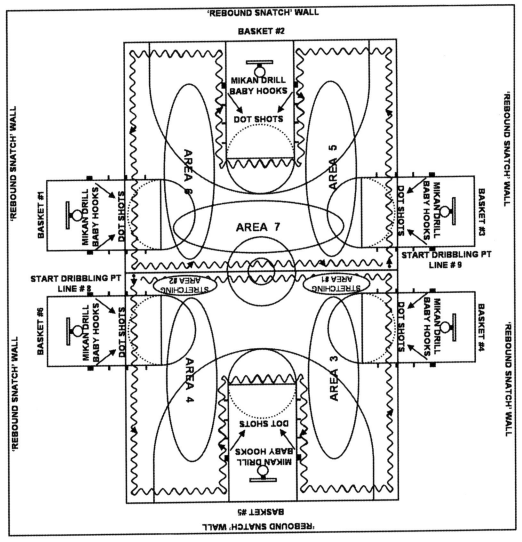

Diagram 7.1

drills/activities to be performed (Diagram 7.1). The time of each drill can be kept by a manager or an assistant coach. A whistle or air-horn can be used to mark the end of each drill. One effective way is to have the scoreboard clock set at 42 minutes and to turn it on at the beginning of the entire routine. A manager can then buzz the horn at the end of each drill/activity to signal the transition from one drill to the next.

Each drill/activity is given a specific location in which it should be practiced. Descriptions of each drill follow, but you should substitute your own drills that meet the space and time requirements of the overall routine.

Using the score clock, the routine starts with 42:00 on the clock. While the varsity squad is spending the first five minutes stretching in areas 1, 2, 3, and 4, the junior varsity squad will be using the two dribbling lines (areas 8 and 9) and all six baskets.

During the next four minutes (beginning with 37:00 on the clock), the varsity will use all six baskets and the areas near those baskets (along with area 7), while the junior varsity use areas 3, 4, 5, and 6.

With 33:00 on the clock, the varsity breaks down with the first six-man squad in area 7 and each individual player of the second six-man squad going to an assigned basket for one minute. The JV squad uses areas 3 and 4 for this single minute.

Beginning at 32:00, the varsity spends the next three minutes in areas 3, 4, 5, and 6, working on pivoting and passing techniques, while the JV breaks down into two-man groups and uses the six baskets to work on the various types of dot shots.

At 29:00, the varsity moves to the two dribbling lines to work on two minutes of dribbling techniques. They then move in pairs to the six baskets to work on the various power moves to the basket for three minutes. The JV begins their stretching routine for five minutes in areas 1, 2, 3, and 4.

With 24:00 on the clock, the varsity takes areas 3, 4, 5, and 6 for five minutes of rebounding and defensive drills. The JV utilizes area 7, all six baskets, and the wall areas near those baskets to work on the various shooting and rebounding techniques and perform a defensive drill.

With 19:00 on the clock, the varsity uses all six baskets for three minutes to perform the dot shots series of drills, while the JV uses areas 3, 4, 5, and 6 to work on the three pivot and pass techniques.

At 16:00, the entire varsity and junior varsity teams group-work for three minutes on a defensive interception drill in their respective half-court areas. After that, the varsity uses areas 3 and 4 to work on some offensive screening techniques for two minutes, while the junior varsity uses areas 5 and 6 to work on the same drills.

At 11:00, both the entire varsity and junior varsity teams again group in their respective half-court locations for four minutes to work on defensive boxing out and offensive rebounding techniques.

With 07:00 on the clock, both teams remain in their respective half-court areas to go cross-court for seven minutes for the so-called full-court drills. When the clock runs down to 0:00, those three full-court drills are concluded, as is the entire 42-minute routine. A positive and enthusiastic tone and attitude has been established for the regular practice for the day.

This is an excellent drill for pre-season training as well as pre-practice training. During the season, when time is of the essence, you can replace some of the fundamental drills, and perhaps even shorten the number of fundamental drills and times with more pertinent team offensive and defensive drills.

Offensive and Shooting Drills

To win games, a team must be able to score. To be able to score, a team must be able to shoot the basketball. As important as accurate and successful shooting is to man-to-man offenses, it is much more so to zone offenses. Many opponents will sometimes play zone defenses because they feel that an offensive team cannot effectively shoot the basketball on a consistent basis. Therefore, offensive/shooting drills and primary shooting drills must be utilized to an even greater degree when working on zone offenses. To work on zone offense shooting, teams should use a variety of types of shooting drills, with each drill offering somewhat different benefits.

Every shooting drill has definite characteristics, but all must be game-realistic. To make these drills as game-realistic as possible, incorporate as many types of pressures (on the players) as possible. Try to incorporate success and competition pressures—trying to beat other players, other squads, and other opponents. The so-called *other opponents* can be pre-set standards or the clock. Obviously, you should stress accuracy in all of your shooting drills, but you should also stress quantity. You should want your shooters, passers, and rebounders to always go at game speed. Continually accelerate your rebounders, passers, and shooters in each and every one of your shooting drills. Have pre-set quantity *and* quality standards for each shooting drill you use. This technique increases the game realism because each individual is trying to succeed not only for himself, but also for his team (or group or squad). Every shooting drill has a pre-set number of attempts he must take, as well as a standard of how many shots he should make. Again, doing so forces the tempo and intensity level to increase for each shooting drill used.

Game realism also means rewards for winning and penalties for not winning. None of the penalties should be harsh or hard, but they should be true penalties. They could be some type of a running penalty or some push-ups or sit-ups. Competing against the clock is always beneficial because everyone then has a common opponent. Using the scoreboard clock not only gives everyone a common opponent, but a clear, visible, and constant opponent. Using time limits always speeds up the shooting groups and it does not allow a player to take too much time in shooting. Use the phrase, "Be quick, but don't be in a hurry." When during a game does a shooter, passer, or any player have the luxury to take his time and to go at a comfortable speed? By continually accelerating your players in all drills (not just when shooting), you get players used to having a much quicker, comfortable speed. Every drill must also be as time-efficient as possible because you cannot afford to waste any practice time.

To achieve such efficiency, incorporate other offensive techniques and fundamentals into each shooting drill, such as passing, rebounding, cutting, coming off of screens, catching, and pivoting. Incorporate the spots where your players will most likely get those shots in games, as well as the types of passes you will have to use in games. Also, place your passers where they will pass the ball from in game situations. Start your shooters in their initial locations and require them to cut and break to the spots where they most likely will take shots during games. Force the passers to quickly and accurately make the appropriate passes that they will make in a game. Sometimes have managers or coaches have their hands up in front of the shooters to act as dummy defenders. Constantly motivate your rebounders to aggressively offensively rebound the basketball before making quick and accurate outlet passes as they would in a real game. If the speed and intensity needed are constantly emphasized, other drills that follow in that day's practice will naturally pick up the same speed and intensity levels that are required for those drills to be successful. Another by-product of these shooting drills can be conditioning. If everyone works at meeting the quantity and quality standards that have been set, each player's physical conditioning will also improve.

In the many different drills that incorporate the 55-second offensive/shooting drill theme, three players are involved. One player is the designated passer, one the designated shooter, and one is the designated rebounder. After 55-seconds, all three players rotate over one position designation and the drill is executed again. The transition of the three-player rotation should take no more than five seconds. In three short minutes, each player receives almost one minute of concentrated work on each of the offensive skills of passing, catching, shooting, rebounding, and outlet passing. The best rotation is from passer to shooter to rebounder and then on to a different shooting location where the three-man rotation starts again. It is important to note that this drill is called the 55-second offensive/shooting drill to demonstrate not only that the drill lasts 55-seconds before a rotation, but also to emphasize that the drill is not just a shooting drill. In a shooting-only drill, the remaining two players are not as important and do not need to work as hard at the various fundamentals they should practice. On

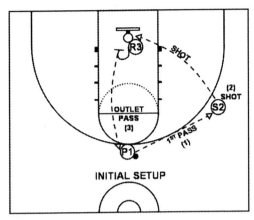

Diagram 7.2

the contrary, all three players in this drill are equally important and should be working equally hard (Diagram 7.2).

S2 takes the shot from an area he will be shooting from while using your zone offense. R3 rebounds the shot, made or missed, and outlet passes to P1. This outlet pass should be to the area where you intend to begin your primary break. P1 passes to S2 who takes his second shot (Diagram 7.2). This continues for 55-seconds. After 55-seconds, S2 becomes R3, R3 rotates to P1 and P1 becomes the new shooter, S2. After the next 55- seconds, each player rotates one more position. After 3 minutes, all three players switch sides of the court to continue for an additional 3 minutes of offensive technique work.

The locations of the shooters and passers can vary to fit the specific offense's needs, while the rebounders obviously always remain near the basket to grab the rebound, outside pivot, and make the outlet pass to the passer. Diagrams 7.3 through 7.7 illustrate just some of the possible combinations of passing and shooting locations. Diagram 7.3 drills on the point to wing pass and an outlet pass. Diagram 7.4 drills on the skip pass and the outlet pass. Diagram 7.5 works on the down pass and the outlet pass and Diagram 7.6 drills on the up-pass. Diagram 7.7 works on the inside pass and the outlet pass. All five 55-second shooting drills accomplish a designated player (R) working on offensive rebounding and outlet passing. The designated passer (P) works on receiving the outlet pass and then making the designated type of pass from the same location he normally would in a game. The designated shooter (S) practices the skills and techniques of catching and quickly shooting from the area he would do so in a game.

The following offensive/shooting drills and primary shooting drills are described in detail, along with the required number of shot attempts and makes your players should have for each specific shooting drill.

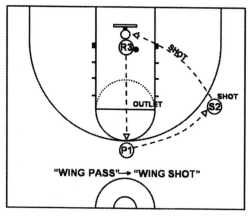

Diagram 7.3

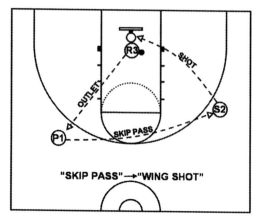

Diagram 7.4

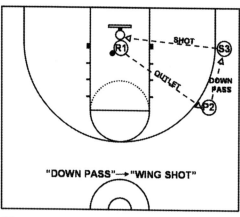

Diagram 7.5

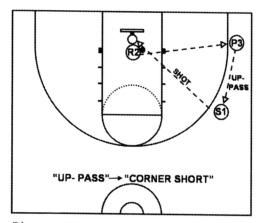

Diagram 7.6

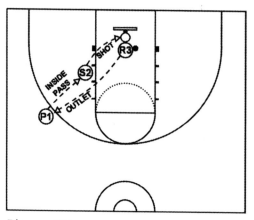

Diagram 7.7

100 Series Drills: Timed Shooting Drills (One to Five Minutes)

The coach should first decide on the zone offenses he intends to employ for a particular season. The coach can then decide on the shooting area for each of his shooters. The shooter should use that area during the shooting drills. Of course, there can be more than one area of the court assigned to a shooter. In that case, the shooter should alternate days shooting from his different assigned areas.

Each 100 series drill is primarily a shooting drill with the main emphasis being on the shooter. The passer makes passes from a specific area to a shooter, who is restricted to a particular shooting area. The shooter catches the pass and takes a shot as quickly as possible. The passer then rebounds the ball and outlet passes the ball back to the shooter who continues the drill. After the designated time limit, the players switch assignments. The number of shot attempts and made baskets are counted and recorded for each shooter from each assigned area.

Drill 101 (Diagram 7.8)

- One ball, two players
- Off of the pass—inside shots (shots in the paint)
- A total of three minutes should yield 27 to 30 shots taken per shooter.
- 70 percent accuracy would be about 19 to 21 shots made; 60 percent accuracy would be about 16 to 18 shots made; 50 percent accuracy would be about 14 to 15 shots made.

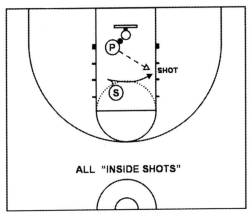

Diagram 7.8

Drill 102 (Diagram 7.9)

- One ball, two players
- Off of the pass—outside shots (outside of the free-throw lane, but inside of the three-point line)
- A total of three minutes should yield 24 to 27 shots taken per shooter.
- 50 percent accuracy would be about 12 to 14 shots made.

Drill 103 (Diagram 7.10)

- One ball, two players
- Off of the pass—three-point shots
- A total of three minutes should yield 21 to 24 shots taken per shooter.
- 50 percent accuracy would be about 10 to 12 shots made.

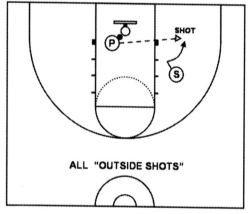

ALL "OUTSIDE SHOTS"

Diagram 7.9

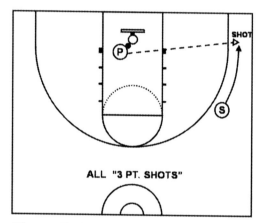

ALL "3 PT. SHOTS"

Diagram 7.10

200 Series Drills: Closeout Shooting Drills Off of the Pass

Like the 100 series, the 200 series drills focus on the shooters. The passer (O1) makes passes from a specific area to a shooter (O2) who is restricted to a designated area. The initial passer then follows his pass and closes out on the initial shooter, putting token defensive pressure on him. The initial passer remains in that area to become the next shooter. The initial shooter catches the pass (already having his feet and hands ready), takes a shot as quickly as possible, then follows his shot and rebounds the ball. He then outlet passes the ball back to the new shooter (thereby becoming the new passer) and closes out and applies token pressure on the new shooter. The two players continue the drill, continually reversing roles. The number of attempts and made baskets are counted and recorded for each shooter from each assigned area. You will note the only difference between the 100 series and the 200 series is the shooter rebounds his own shot before passing to another shooter in the 200 series, while one shooter took all the shots in the 100 series. You would want to use the 100 series when a need for one shooter to work on his shot exists. You would want to use the 200 series as a change or when you want two similar shooters working on their shots at the same time.

Drill 201 (Diagram 7.11)

- One ball, two players, and rotation
- Off of the pass—inside shots (inside of the free-throw lane)
- A total of three minutes should yield 37 to 39 shots taken by each shooter.
- 70 percent accuracy would be about 26 to 27 shots made; 60 percent accuracy would be about 22 to 23 shots made; 50 percent accuracy would be about 18 to 20 shots made.

Drill 202 (Diagram 7.12)

- One ball, two players, and rotation
- Off of the pass—outside shots
- A total of three minutes should yield 35 to 37 shots taken by each shooter.
- 60 percent accuracy would be about 21 to 22 shots made; 50 percent accuracy would be about 18 shots made.

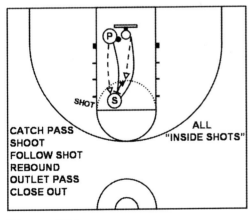

Diagram 7.11

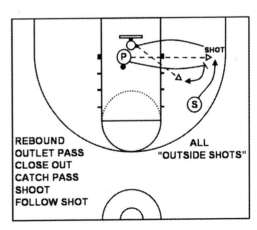

Diagram 7.12

Drill 203 (Diagram 7.13)

- One ball, two players, and rotation
- Off of the pass—three-point shots
- A total of three minutes should yield 28 to 32 shots taken by each shooter.
- 50 percent accuracy would be 14 to 16 shots made.

Drill 204 (Diagram 7.14)

- Rapid fire with two balls, three players, and rotation
- Off of the pass—outside shots or three-point shots
- A total of three minutes should yield 26 to 28 shots for each of the three shooters.
- 50 percent accuracy would be about 13 to 14 shots made.
- The first passer (O1) passes the ball to the first shooter (O3) and closes out on that shooter. That shooter (O3) shoots and follows the shot to become the third passer. As this takes place, the second passer (O2) passes the ball to the first passer (O1), who now is the second shooter. The second shooter (O1) catches the pass, shoots, and follows his shot to become the fourth passer. The drill continues for the set time limit, with all three players being passers as well as shooters/rebounders.

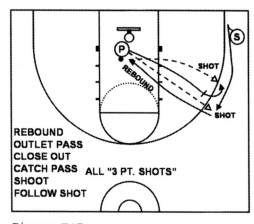

Diagram 7.13

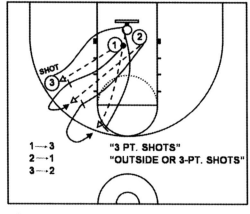

Diagram 7.14

300 Series Drills

The 300 series drills feature both the shooters and passers with very important points of emphasis. The passer makes passes from a specific area to a shooter that is restricted to a particular area. The passer follows his pass and closes out on the shooter, putting more token defensive pressure on the shooter. The shooter then must make a realistic shot-fake and drive past the defender (scraping off of the defender on alternate sides of him), toward the basket with a pre-designated number of dribbles, before finally shooting the ball. A second shot-fake against a second token defender may be required before the actual shot is taken. After the closeout, the initial passer remains in the shooting area to become the next shooter, while the initial shooter follows his shot so that he can rebound and then become the new passer. The two (or possibly three) players continue the drill, changing back and forth from being passers and defenders to becoming shooters. The number of attempts and made baskets are counted and recorded for each shooter from each assigned shooting area. You will note the 300 series incorporates the shot off the dribble. To review: 100 series has only one shooter, 200 series has two (three) shooters, and the 300 series brings the same drill but includes shots off the dribble (with fakes). Coaches must decide before each practice which of the series they want for that particular practice.

Drill 301 (Diagram 7.15)

- One ball, two players
- Shooters should fake a three-pointer, drive, and then take an outside shot. Shooters should change directions and the number of dribbles.
- A total of three minutes should yield 33 to 35 shots attempted by each shooter.
- 60 percent accuracy would be about 20 shots made; 50 percent accuracy would be about 16 to 18 shots made.

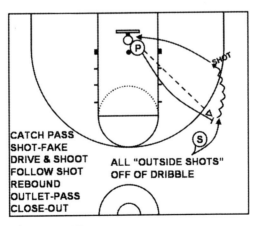

Diagram 7.15

Drill 302 (Diagram 7.16)

- One ball, two players

- The shooter (S) should fake an outside shot, drive by the closeout defender (D), and take a power shot. He should change the direction he takes and the number of dribbles used. The shooter can stop, pump fake, then shoot at the end of the dribble; or, the shooter can stop, ball fake, use an up and under, or similar inside move at the end of the dribble.

- A total of three minutes should yield 30 to 32 shots taken by each shooter.

- 70 percent accuracy would be about 21 to 22 shots made; 60 percent accuracy would be about 18 to 19 shots made.

Drill 303 (Diagram 7.17)

- One ball, three players, and rotation

- The shooter (S) must first always make a good shot-fake, then dribble-scrape off of the closeout defender (P), and make a power move at the second token defender (D), using between one and three dribbles.

- The rotation of players could be P to S to D to P.

- A total of three minutes should yield about 20 shot attempts for each of the three shooters.

- 60 percent accuracy would be about 12 shots made; 50 percent accuracy would be about 10 shots made.

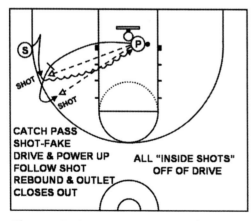

CATCH PASS
SHOT-FAKE
DRIVE & POWER UP
FOLLOW SHOT
REBOUND & OUTLET
CLOSES OUT

ALL "INSIDE SHOTS"
OFF OF DRIVE

Diagram 7.16

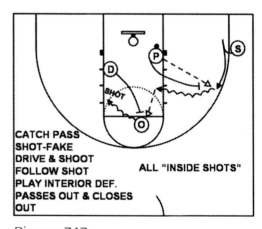

CATCH PASS
SHOT-FAKE
DRIVE & SHOOT
FOLLOW SHOT
PLAY INTERIOR DEF.
PASSES OUT & CLOSES
OUT

ALL "INSIDE SHOTS"

Diagram 7.17

Drill 304 (Diagram 7.18)

- One ball, four players, and rotation
- The shooter (S) first must catch the pass, make a realistic shot-fake, and scrape off the closeout defender (D) by taking between one and three dribbles toward the basket. On his drive to the basket, he should drive and dish to a second offensive player (O), who then takes an inside shot versus the defender (D) who is waiting in the lane. This drill can be adjusted to include the freeze dribble (or the gap dribble) by putting two defenders in the drill (one on the dribbler). These shooting drills are building blocks for an effective zone offense.
- A total of four minutes should yield approximately 14 to 16 shots for each of the four shooters.
- 70 percent accuracy would be about nine to 11 shots made; 60 percent accuracy would be about eight to 10 shots made.
- The rotation of players could be P to S to D to O to P.

Drill 305 (Diagram 7.19)

- One ball, four players, and rotation
- The shooter (S) first catches the pass from the passer/closeout defender (P) and makes a good shot fake. He then takes one to three dribbles toward the basket and should penetrate and pitch to a second offensive player (O) outside the line, who then takes a three-point shot versus the second defender (D), who closes out on him from the lane.
- The rotation of players could also be P to S to D to O to P.
- A total of four minutes should yield 10 to 12 shots for each shooter.
- 50 percent accuracy would be about five shots made; 40 percent accuracy would be about four shots made.

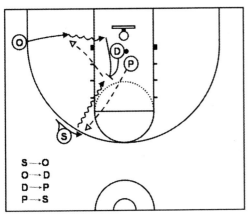

Diagram 7.18

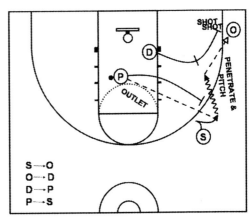

Diagram 7.19

Drill 306 (Diagram 7.20)

- Rapid fire with two balls, three players, and rotation

- The first passer (P1) passes the ball and closes out on the first shooter (S) while the first shooter shot-fakes, then drives toward the basket before taking an outside jump shot. The first passer (P1) then becomes the next shooter for the next passer (P2).

- The rotation of players could be P1 to S to P2 to P1.

- A total of three minutes should yield about 24 shot attempts for each shooter.

- 60 percent accuracy would be about 14 shots made; 50 percent accuracy would be about 12 shots made for each of the three shooters.

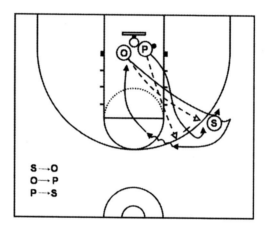

Diagram 7.20

Rapid Fire 55-Second Shooting Drill

This drill is primarily for the shooters and utilizes two non-shooters acting as combination rebounders/passers (P1 and P2). Both retrieve their ball that the shooter (S) has shot and quickly pass it back to the shooter. With two basketballs in play, the shooter must quickly take one shot, then instantly get his feet and hands ready to catch the second ball and quickly shoot again. This continues for 55-seconds before a new shooter is designated and the remaining two players become the rebounders/passers. This drill is intense and provides a concentrated amount of shooting by each participant. This drill really forces the shooter to get prepared to catch and shoot, then quickly recover and be ready to shoot again.

Drill 501 (Diagram 7.21)

- Two balls, three players

- The players are given the following roles: shooter (S), rebounder/passer (P1), and rebounder/passer (P2).

- All shots should be taken quickly off of the pass, with two players acting as a combination of rebounder and passer. Make sure shooters shoot from spots they will shoot from in games within the framework of the zone offense.

- Three minutes should yield 22–24 shot attempts for each shooter.

- 60 percent accuracy would be about 13 to 14 shots made; 50 percent accuracy would be about 11 to 12 shots made.

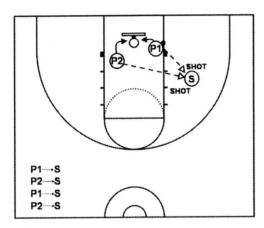

Diagram 7.21

600 Series Drills: Power Shots

The 600 series drills are primarily shooting drills designed for all players to work on catching the ball in the paint and then applying the post player's power moves against a token post defense. The token post defense probably should use the bubble pads to bump the offensive player during the drill. There can be a designated post player (S), a passer (P), and a defender (X) in these drills. After two minutes, all three players rotate, with the passer becoming the post player, the post player becoming the new defender, and the defender becoming the new passer. Each side of the lane should be worked for half of the two-minute shooting segment. Another way of applying these shooting drills for post players is to make them one-man drills. That one player tosses the ball out in front to himself (as if it were a bounce pass). He catches the pass and imagines where the defender is and makes the appropriate move depending upon where the imaginary post defender is positioned. As he catches the ball, he should take a small hop and land on both feet at the same time. Doing so allows him to be able to use either foot as the pivot foot. Two post-players (one on each side of the lane) can operate at the same time at each basket. Again, the shooter goes for a two-minute time period before the drill concludes.

Drill 601: Show and Go Opposite Drop-Step Power Moves (Diagram 7.22)

- These moves should be made toward the middle as well as toward the baseline.
- These moves should start on the first notch above the block on both sides of the lane.
- The post player's fakes should be realistic and come before he actually makes his drop-step move to the basket (in the opposite direction of the fake).
- Two minutes should yield a total of 20 shot attempts for each shooter.
- 80 percent accuracy would be 16 shots made; 60 percent accuracy would be 12 shots made; 50 percent accuracy would be 10 shots made.

Drill 602: Square up, Up-and-Under Crossover Power Moves (Diagram 7.23)

- The post player's fakes should be realistic and come before he actually squares up to the basket and makes his up-and-under move to the basket.

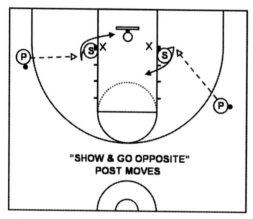

"SHOW & GO OPPOSITE"
POST MOVES

Diagram 7.22

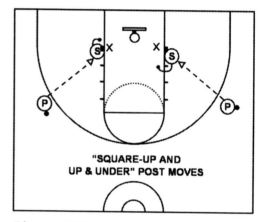

"SQUARE-UP AND
UP & UNDER" POST MOVES

Diagram 7.23

Drill 603: Whirl Moves (Hakeem Olajuwon Moves) (Diagram 7.24)

- These spin or whirl moves should be made toward the baseline and also toward the middle. They also should be initiated from both sides of the lane.

Drill 604: One-Man Dot Shots

- This drill is done with only a shooter (no passer or defender).
- . Version A: With no fakes and no dribble (Diagram 7.25)
- Version B: With one fake and one dribble (Diagram 7.26)
- Version C: With two fakes and one or two dribbles (Diagram 7.27)

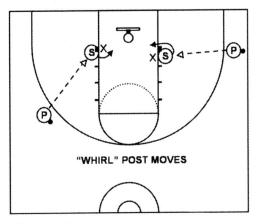

"WHIRL" POST MOVES

Diagram 7.24

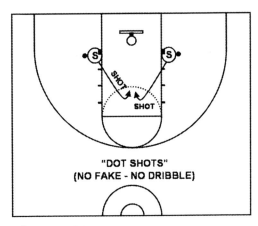

"DOT SHOTS"
(NO FAKE - NO DRIBBLE)

Diagram 7.25

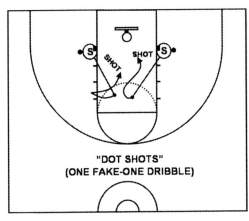

"DOT SHOTS"
(ONE FAKE-ONE DRIBBLE)

Diagram 7.26

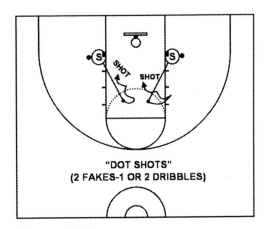

"DOT SHOTS"
(2 FAKES-1 OR 2 DRIBBLES)

Diagram 7.27

Drill 605: Mikan Drill and Baby Hooks Drills (One-Man Drills)

Version A (Diagram 7.28)

- The Mikan drill is a continuous lay-up drill with no dribbles involved, using the left and the right hand on the respective sides of the basket.

- One minute should yield about 15 shot attempts.

- 80 percent accuracy would be 12 made lay-ups.

Version B (Diagram 7.29)

- The baby hooks shooting drill is a continuous very short hook-shot shooting drill, with either one or no dribbles involved, using the left and the right hand on the respective sides of the basket.

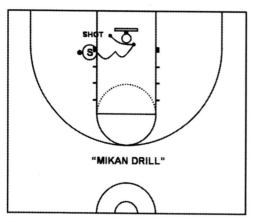

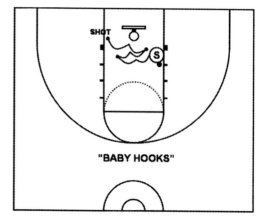

Diagram 7.28

Diagram 7.29

Drill 606: Drop-Step Power Move (One Man Drill) (Diagram 7.30)

- This drill calls for the player to duck-in to the dotted circle in the middle of the free-throw lane, rip-step through the (imaginary) defense, and perform drop-step power moves to the basket (coming from both the left and right blocks).

- This drill is a continuous power-move drill, with one dribble involved, using the appropriate drop-steps toward the baseline coming from the respective sides of the basket.

Drill 607: Spin Screen shots from the Secondary Break (One-Man Drill) (Diagram 7.31)

- This drill works on the preliminary footwork that eventually leads to receiving the spin screen (imaginary in the case of this drill), before receiving the pass (from the shooter himself in this drill), and concluding with a drop-step toward the baseline and a power-move shot.

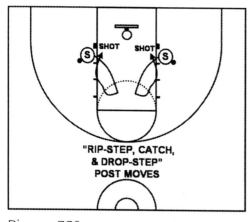

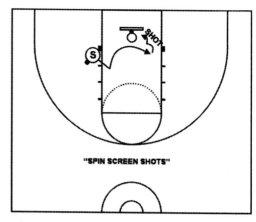

Diagram 7.30

Diagram 7.31

800 Series Drill: 40 Shooting Contest

This shooting drill is a one-on-one competition drill based on shooting quickness and accuracy from five different areas that have three different ranges—three-point range, outside-shot range, lay-up/power-shot range—and a free-throw shooting spot. One shooter starts with jump shots from the five different areas and finishes with five free throws, while the other shooter starts with free throws and finishes with jump shots from the five different areas. Points are awarded only for made shots. After each shot, the shooter must follow his shot, retrieve the ball, then dribble the ball to the next spot in the particular area that he is shooting from, and then take the jump shot (or power shot from the lane). The first shooter to finish the drill gets five points: made three-point shots are worth three points each, made two-point jump shots are worth two points, and made power shots and made free throws are worth one point each. Therefore, each area has a maximum of six points if all three shots are made. Making all three shots from each of the five areas, making all five free throws, and finishing first would give the shooter the maximum of 40 points.

Drill 801 (Diagram 7.32)

- Two balls, two players
- It should take three minutes for both shooters to complete the drill.
- Select any five different spots on the court (outside the three-point line).
- The shooter ball-fakes and drives for a driving power inside shot (worth one point). He then takes one shot from behind the line (three points). He then ball-fakes and takes an outside shot (two points). At some point, each shooter takes five consecutive free throws (one point).
- The direction of the fakes and the number of dribbles taken should be designated by the coaching staff and should change often.

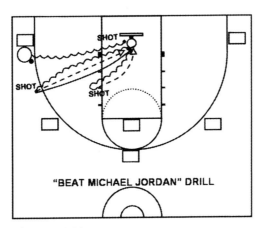

Diagram 7.32

1000 Series Drill: Follow Your Shot Shooting Drill

This shooting drill is similar to the 200 series closeout shooting drills in that it has a defender closing out to put some pressure on the perimeter shooter. The difference between the drills comes after the initial catch and perimeter shot off of the pass against defensive pressure. At that point, the shooter must follow his shot, offensive rebound, and take a stick-back shot. He then becomes a passer and eventually a defensive player who closes out on another perimeter shooter. This three-minute shooting drill starts with two passers underneath the basket. The first passer (O1) passes it out to the first shooter (O3) and closes out with his hands up. The first shooter (O3) catches the pass and then shoots and follows his own shot with a stick-back (regardless of whether the initial shot was made or missed). As the first stick-back takes place, the first passer (O1) squares up and receives a pass from the second passer (O2), who then closes out on the first passer (O1, the new shooter). This rotation continues. The shooting spots for each player should correspond to the spots where that player will take shots off the zone offense you intend to use.

Drill 1001 (Diagram 7.33)

- Two balls, three players
- The accuracy-level goals vary for each individual shooter.
- The outlet pass should not be made until the stick-back is being shot.
- Three minutes should yield 15 shots of both kinds for each shooter.

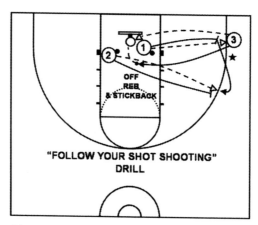

Diagram 7.33

1200 Series Drill: Solo Shooting Drill

This drill is strictly a shooting drill with competition between each individual player. After each shot (after an initial pass to himself), the shooter must hustle to retrieve the ball, and then quickly dribble out to the same designated spot where he started to take his next shot. He does not take a stick-back shot in this drill; instead, he repeats the shot by dribbling out to the same location and shooting from there. He must dribble quickly with his head up, so that he does not run into one of the other three participating players at that basket. The coaching staff should designate the four locations where the four shooters are to shoot from and determine whether the shooters can take one or two dribbles before shooting or pass the ball to themselves (so that the shooter can work on shooting off of the pass). The coaching staff designates penalties for the losing individuals. Each shooter must keep track of his made jump shots and call out his new score after every made jumper. After each 55-second period, each shooter rotates to the next location to his right. This transition should take no more than five seconds and the drill restarts for another 55-seconds. The 55-second shooting period is for each of the five shooting spots, with the entire drill lasting five minutes.

Drill 1201 (Diagram 7.34)

- One ball per player, maximum of five shooters at each basket
- Each player shoots a jump shot and follows his shot to retrieve the ball. He then dribbles out to that same spot on the same side of the floor to take the next jump shot off of the dribble or after a pass to himself.
- The goal is to take six to eight shots per minute.

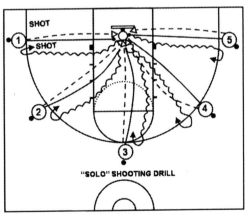

Diagram 7.34

- Every shooter then rotates to the next spot to repeat the drill at a different spot.

- It should take five minutes for each shooter to shoot at all five designated spots and take about 30 to 40 shots.

- This is a great drill to end practice, leaving the squad feeling in a good mood, yet working on the spots of the zone offense.

Offensive Dribbling and Passing Breakdown Drills

The basic offensive fundamentals of dribbling and passing are probably more important to a successful zone offense than they are in a man offense. Working diligently on these offensive fundamentals is a must to make a zone offense better prepared, and it will also benefit a team in their man offense. Therefore, these skills should be worked on quite often in daily practices.

Diagram 7.35 illustrates the zone offense combo passing drill, which can be incorporated with just six players and two managers or coaches. Players work on making three types of passes that will be used often during games against zone defenses. Two players (O5 and O2) work on making and receiving skip passes. Another player (O1) works on making inside passes to a post player (O6), with that post player then working on making kick-out passes back to a different perimeter location (O3). That perimeter player (O3) works on making wing passes to another perimeter player (O4) on the wing. After 55-seconds, the passers and the pass receivers can rotate to switch assignments. After all players have worked on the designated passing, the location of the passer and the pass receiver can also change. These six players can easily work this drill in a half-court setting, with another six players working on something else at a different basket.

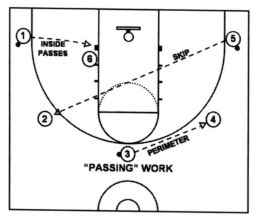

Diagram 7.35

Don't just drill for drills sake. Make sure all passers and receivers are in their playing positions of your chosen zone offenses. Make sure the drills are game-realistic, incorporating pressure, competition, and game speed.

Diagram 7.36 illustrates a drill in which players work on techniques, freeze dribbling at defenders before making a pass to a teammate. Two defenders (A and B) and one pass receiver (O4) are needed in addition to the players (O1, O2, and O3) who are working on their designated dribbling skills and techniques. Six players can easily work this drill in a half-court setting, with the remaining six players working on something else at a different basket.

In this drill, O1 dribble drives toward XA. Because XB began guarding O1, XA will follow O1, and XA must deny O1 dribble penetration; hence, XA is frozen. O4 can square up for a shot as he receives a pass from O1. Players rotate from O1 to XB to XA to O4 to end of the line (Diagram 7.36).

Diagram 7.37 illustrates another drill for eight offensive players to work on the skills and techniques of the all-important pull dribbles. This group of players can work at one half-court setting in the three most common areas in which the pull dribble is utilized— the deep-corner areas and the top of the key. A pass receiver is needed to receive the pass after the pull dribble is made from each of the three areas, along with a flash post player who replaces the original post player. Four defenders are also needed to provide game realism. All players should take their necessary repetitions to improve their dribbling, passing, flash-cutting, and pass-catching techniques.

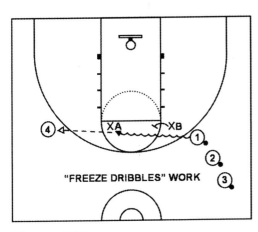

Diagram 7.36

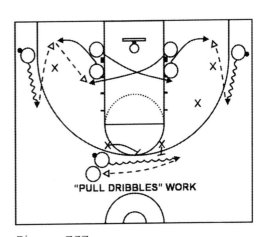

Diagram 7.37

Diagram 7.38 illustrates another drill for players to not work only on learning and understanding the concepts of gap dribbling, but also on improving the techniques, skills, and methods of gap dribbles. Three groups of four players can work at one half-court setting. A pass receiver is needed to receive the pass after the gap dribble is made. Two defenders are needed in each of the three groups for the operation of this drill and to improve game realism and effectiveness. Six offensive players and two managers are also involved in the drill. The drill should be as time-efficient as possible. After a designated time elapses (such as the typical 55-seconds), each player can rotate to a new position.

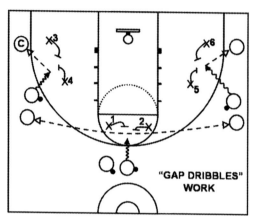

Diagram 7.38

Offensive Pivoting, Passing, and Catching Breakdown Drills

Another invaluable offensive fundamental that is needed for a team to be successful in the execution of any offense (both man and zone) is pivoting away from or around individual defensive pressure and then delivering the ball to an open teammate. This technique works against man-to-man pressure, half-court zone or trap pressure, or full-court defensive pressure. Teams must be able to move the ball both on the perimeter as well as to the inside to constantly attack an opponent's defense against the various zone defenses.

Start this invaluable drill only after instilling the attitude to all players that it is a multi-purpose drill needed for each player to become a well-rounded and fundamentally sound basketball player. Use this drill in your pre-practice fundamental and stretching routine. Because it is such a time-efficient drill and because it encompasses so many different fundamentals, you can (and should) utilize this drill in your practice sessions more than once a day.

The pass receivers (O3, O6, O9, O12 in Diagram 7.39) work first on the pre-catch and pre-shooting stance. The coaching staff should constantly emphasize to the (potential) shooter, "Get your feet and hands ready... get behind the ball...give the passer a target!" Even before the actual catch of the basketball, you want the pass receiver to already have his inside shoulder (i.e., the shoulder closest to the basket) facing the basket and to have his guide hand up as if he is already shooting the ball. The actual shooting hand should also be in position as if the shooter has already caught the ball and is about to shoot. With the shooting hand in that position, the pass receiver can easily give a target to the passer. The pass receiver should always pivot off of the heel of his inside foot (i.e., the foot closest to the basket). If the pass receiver is in a stationary position, he can start with the inside heel already touching the floor and the rest of that foot not yet touching the floor. If the pass receiver is on the move, he might have to chop up his steps to time the inside heel hitting the floor (to pivot) just as the ball hits the palm of the shooting hand. From there, the heel being planted first will stop the pass receiver's forward momentum of his cut toward the passer. After his shot, you want the shooter to be able to rise straight up and come back straight down without floating in either direction. Stopping all of the momentum from the shooter's cut before he shoots the ball will make the shooter much more accurate. Each shooter shoots as if the original passer is the basket, so that the ball is returned for that passer to restart working on his skills and techniques.

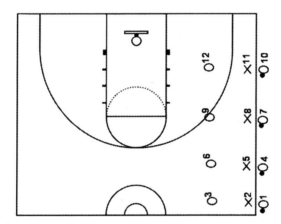

Diagram 7.39

Once the momentum is stopped, the heel actually will allow for a smooth, easy, and complete pivot toward the basket, as the shooter swings his free (i.e., outside) foot and leg around so that he is completely squared up to the basket. In this particular drill, the pass receiver/shooter shoots the ball at an imaginary basket back to the original passer. The passer is now quickly ready to resume working on his technique of passing to the shooter again, so that the shooter can quickly work on the foot and handwork part of his shooting technique.

The men in the middle of the drill (X2, X5, X9, and X12 in Diagram 7.39) utilize the drill as a defensive drill, as they are initially guarding the dribbler/passer. Emphasize defensive fundamentals (such as proper stance and other various defensive techniques), as they should not be taken lightly by players or the coaching staff. Remember, this drill is also a defensive fundamental drill. These defensive players work on defensive techniques only on the original dribbler/passer and not on the pass receiver/shooter.

The dribbler/passers (O1, O4, O7, and O10 in Diagram 7.39) work on the dribbling, pivoting, and passing techniques and skills that are required for him to be a solid all-around offensive player. The first technique to be worked on is the actual dribble as the dribbler approaches the defender. Dribbling quickly (but in a very controlled manner) in a semi-crouch stance with the head up is the first point of emphasis for the offensive player. Have players practice using both hands to dribble. The primary passing hand is the second major point of emphasis.

Step 1 of the Pivot and Pass Technique

As the dribbler approaches the defender and kills his dribble, the dribbler should take a small bunny hop and land simultaneously on both feet. Doing so allows him to use either foot as the pivot foot (Diagram 7.40).

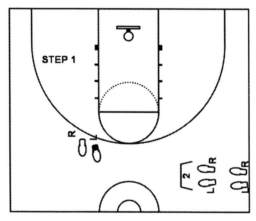

Diagram 7.40

Step 2 of the Pivot and Pass Technique

If the passer wants to attack the defender by passing laterally around the defender's left side, the dribbler should land and make his left foot the pivot foot. Doing so makes the passer's right foot his free foot, which can laterally step toward the outside of the defender's left foot (Diagram 7.41). As this is taking place, the passer should protect the ball by firmly holding it with both hands with the ball held behind the knee of the free foot (i.e., the right knee in this example). If the passer's free foot is laterally outside the defender's foot, the passer then could fake low and go high or fake high and go low (i.e., passing high over the defender's left hand or passing low under the defender's hand). Constantly tell the dribbler-turned-passer to protect the ball behind the knee and to step due east or due west, which is to say that the dribbler/passer should constantly attack the flanks of the defender by stepping laterally around him.

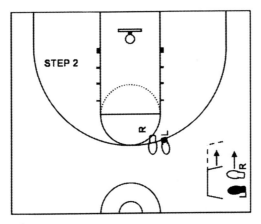

Diagram 7.41

Step 3 of the Pivot and Pass Technique

If the defender counters the dribbler's first lateral attack, have the dribbler rip the ball low and hard across his shoe tops as he steps with a front pivot across the face of the defender to laterally attack the defender on the opposite side (in this scenario, it is the defender's right side). The ball ends up on the inside of the knee of the passer's free leg (the right knee in this example) (Diagram 7.42). If the passer's free foot (right) gets outside the defender's (right) foot, the passer looks to pass the ball around the defender (fake high and go low or fake low and go high) on the opposite side from the initial side of attack. Again, strongly emphasize to the pivoting passer to protect the ball behind the free (right) knee and step due west and/or due east in the lateral attacks on the ball defender.

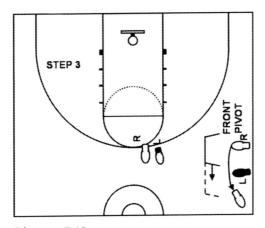

Diagram 7.42

Step 4 of the Pivot and Pass Technique

If the defender reacts quickly and takes this second method of passing away, you should emphasize to the offensive player to remain in the semi-crouch stance, then quickly reverse-pivot off of the same (left) foot and attack the defender's original (left) lateral side. The ball should then be back behind the knee of the free (right) foot. Again, the three main points of emphasis to the passer are the following: protect the basketball by placing the ball behind the free knee, step outside the defender's foot (by going east or west), and fake high and go low or fake low and go high. If the defense counters this third step, the dribbler should reverse pivot and look to make a lesser contested pass to a teammate or attempt to use all three steps again (Diagram 7.43).

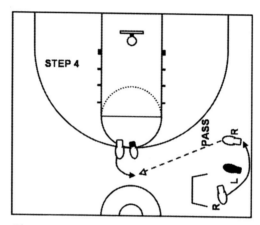

Diagram 7.43

After 55-seconds, the dribbling/pivoting/passing player (O1) switches to the defensive station, while the first defender (X2) switches to work at the pass-receiving/shooting station, and the first pass-receiver/shooter (O3) rotates to the dribbling/pivoting/passing station. This rotation should take less than five seconds and the drill starts again. After the third 55-second period has concluded, you can start the second round with all offensive dribblers using the opposite dribbling hand and making the right foot the new pivot foot. In just six minutes, three players will each have almost two minutes of concentrated work on all three stations—the dribbling, pivoting, and passing phase, the defensive phase, and the pass-catching and shooting phase.

Offensive Rebounding Drills

Many coaches believe that a zone defense forces an offense to take more perimeter shots and that it is more difficult for a zone defensive team to box out and defensive rebound than for a man-to-man defensive team. The more perimeter shots that are taken, the more likely there will be an increase in missed shots. Therefore, offensive rebounding could be considered more valuable in zone offenses than in man offenses. Those missed shots from a zone offense are there for the taking for the zone offensive team, with unsuccessful box-outs and fewer defensive rebounds more likely to take place for the zone defensive team. The zone offensive team must capitalize on that probable advantage.

To make a team more effective in its zone offense attack, coaches must not only work on the shooting skills of the players, but also work on all players' individual offensive rebounding skills. One drill to work on offensive rebounding skills and techniques is a simple competitive two-man drill called the circle box-out drill, which not only works on offensive rebounding techniques, but also defensive box-out techniques.

To begin this drill, coaches should place a basketball in the center of the jump circle at mid-court, with a defender facing out opposite the ball, with his heels on the outer edge of the circle. Coaches should position the offensive rebounder a full step from (and to the outside of) the defender. A coach should yell, "Shot!" The defenders should work on the various methods of boxing out the offensive rebounder, while the offensive rebounders work on techniques of defeating the defensive box-out and utilizing other offensive rebounding skills. The drill is a one-on-one competitive drill with a winner and a loser. If the offensive rebounder can grab (or at least touch) the basketball within a three-second count after the imaginary shot is taken, he is the winner. If the defender prevents the offensive rebounder from making contact with the basketball on the floor within the three-second time limit, the defense wins. Three varying scenarios can be created in which both the offensive and defensive players develop the appropriate techniques. The three scenarios could be that the offensive player acts like he is the actual shooter, the offensive player is just one pass away on the left side or the right side of the imaginary passer/shooter, and the offensive player is more than one pass away from an (imaginary) offensive player who is on the either side of the circle and takes the (imaginary) shot when the coach yells, "Shot!"

The offensive techniques do not vary from one scenario to the other. All three techniques can be used in any of the three shooting scenarios. The three techniques are as follows:

- As the defense makes contact with the offensive rebounder, the offensive rebounder can go butt-to-butt and spin off (the defender) and continue after the basketball.

- The offensive rebounder can use a swim technique to escape the contact of the defensive box-out before hustling to the ball.

- The offensive rebounder can step backwards away from the defensive contact and then slash to the ball after scraping off of the defender on the side opposite of the position where the defender looks for the offensive rebounder.

An example of this third technique is when the offensive rebounder breaks contact with the defender and the defender turns to look over his right shoulder to visibly find the offensive rebounder. The offensive rebounder should then attack the left side of the defender and slash to the ball.

In just a few minutes, both players can have several repetitions, both offensively and defensively. In addition to the center jump circle, each basket that has a free-throw line and a top of the key can be used as a station for this drill. With a maximum of two pairs of players at each of the seven stations, that would then involve a maximum of 28 different players (Diagram 7.44).

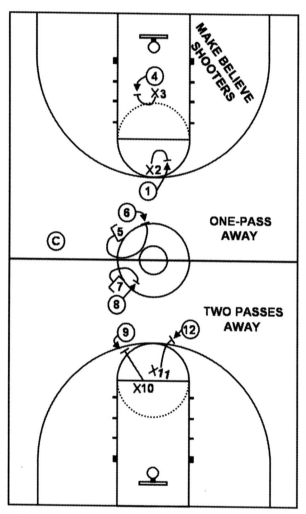

Diagram 7.44

The Transition Drills

A common coaching belief is that to attack an opponent who zones, the offensive team must get down the floor quickly and beat them before they set up their zone defense. Another belief is that zone defenses can and will fast break on your offensive team more effectively. Therefore, the transition from your team's defense to its zone offense should be emphasized. Likewise, the transition from (zone) offense to defense should constantly be stressed to your players. To teach the importance of transition, use game-realistic drills as often as possible. Improved physical conditioning is a by-product of using transition drills frequently, as is the improvement of several offensive fundamentals.

Super Transition Drill

The primary purpose of this drill is to work on your team's transition game, both from offense to defense and from defense to offense. In some cases, both can be worked on simultaneously. In essence, Squad A must compete against two different squads, each with distinct positional advantages over them. Use the overload theory to make the drill extremely difficult for the designated squad. Having the drill tougher than actual game situations should improve performances during games.

The drill can be initiated with a five-on-five controlled scrimmage with a selected team—Squad A—as the coaching staff's primary focus. Coaches should have Squad A run through their offensive entries or offensive continuities against a defensive group (Squad B). Squad A could devote time and effort to improving their transition from offense to defense after losing possession of the basketball, via committing turnovers or after missing or actually making shots. Squad C has absolutely no defensive responsibilities and is stationed in a random manner out near the ten-second line and close to the frontcourt hash marks. Their primary responsibility is to generate a fast break much more quickly than would occur in an ordinary setting. This puts extra pressure on Squad A by overloading the degree of difficulty in their transition to defense.

Defensive Transition after a Turnover

To practice this transition, Squad A aligns in the appropriate offensive set and runs an entry or even gets into an offensive continuity pattern. On the coaching staff's whistle, they instantly drop the ball (as in a turnover). The defensive team (Squad B) then recovers the loose ball and immediately outlets the ball to an assistant coach, who is located near one of the two frontcourt hash marks. That coach hands the ball to a player on Squad C (C1), who initiates his team's fast break at the other end of the court. C1 comes back to receive the handoff and then must dribble the ball all the way to the opposite end of the court, where his teammates have sprinted ahead to run their primary and secondary fast breaks. Team C has a head-start advantage over all the members of Team A, who must sprint back and prevent uncontested shots from being generated from Team C's fast breaks (Diagram 7.45).

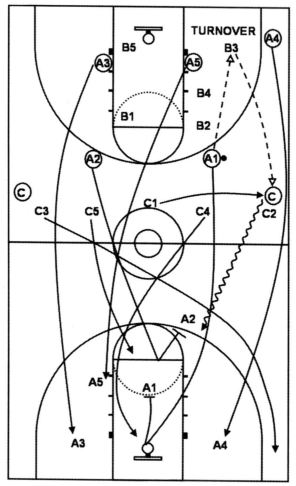

Diagram 7.45

Defensive Transition after a Missed (or Made) Shot

Another scenario calls for Team A to look patiently for a good shot while running their offense. When they finally take a shot, they then look to legitimately offensive rebound the missed shot. To maximize the chance for defensive rebounds, you might want to dictate to the squad to make the effort to rebound, but not allow them to actually grab the offensive rebound. Therefore, all missed shots would result in defensive rebounds. After securing the defensive rebound, Squad B's rebounders could pitch the outlet pass out to C1 so that Squad C could run their offensive fast break (with another head start over Squad A). If Squad A actually makes the shot, the assistant coach on the side of the court could use a new basketball and quickly outlet the ball to C1 again to start an immediate fast break going down court in the opposite direction. Squad A would run their offense, shoot, and make a futile attempt to offensively rebound the shot before then hustling back to stop Squad C's fast break at the other end of the floor.

To make Squad A's task of getting back on defense much more difficult, the supplemental group of players in Squad C could be spread out in a manner that would give them a significant positional advantage over Squad A when getting down court. Obviously, Squad C would have a head start as they sprint out and look for the outlet pass from the assistant coach. The assistant coach pitches the ball out to one of the players on Squad C and that group looks to run their primary fast break (and on into their secondary fast break). Squad A must quickly sprint back from offense to defense (after their missed shot) to defend their basket against the offensive fast breaking (this structure is the same as in Diagram 7.45).

The members of Squad A must sprint back in their defensive fast break lanes as fast as they can to stop the primary fast break (and ultimately the opponent's secondary fast break). Squad C could be instructed to force a shot out of their primary break or the secondary fast break, force a pass that could most likely become a turnover, or remain patient and under control in their offense and look to carefully score in a legitimate manner. Squad A should initially be working on preventing easy shots out of the opponents' primary or secondary fast break (Diagram 7.45). Ultimately, when Squad A is on defense and finally recovers possession of the ball, they quickly reverse their direction and sprint back (from defense) to offense toward their original basket. Squad A will not have any supplemental group to aid them in transition, so they will again run the entire length of the floor and perform both their primary and secondary fast breaks against Squad B, which has the advantage of being able to defensively set up ahead of them. Squad B has gained their advantage by moving toward the ten-second timeline, while Squad C was attacking Squad A (Diagram 7.46). Squad B will easily get back ahead of Squad A. Squad A must execute both their primary and secondary breaks, as well as possibly move into their continuity offense.

As Squad A offensively attacks Squad B, the supplemental group, Squad C, positions itself ready to run another offensive fast break. The cycle is ready to be repeated. Both the B and the C Squads start with positional advantages, and also enjoy a breather while the other squad is competing against Squad A. However, Squad A never has a positional advantage or a breather. This drill is a good example of the overload method. Players should be substituted into Squad A as the drill continues.

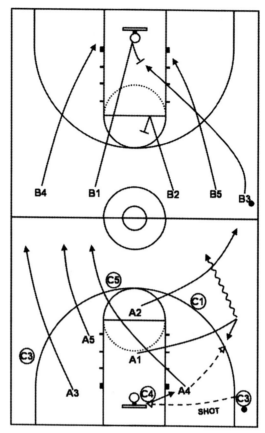

Diagram 7.46

Many benefits are available in this drill for each of the three groups. Squad A will receive work and practice in the following:

- Running a half-court offense.
- Reacting and getting back on defense after turnovers or made/missed shots to prevent easy lay-ups by their opponents.
- Reacting quickly to run their own primary and secondary fast breaks on offense (from a half-court defensive setting).
- A great deal of full-court conditioning as they work on the different aspects of their transition game.

Squad B, meanwhile, will be able to work on their half-court defense as well as the back part of their defense versus an opponent's fast breaks (in a controlled setting). Squad C could be a less talented team (junior varsity or freshmen) that could work on the latter half of their offensive fast breaks (i.e., a little of their primary break as well as their secondary break).

Squads A and B should eventually exchange their original positions so that Squad B receives focused attention and works on their own transition game—both offensive and defensive. This drill requires the full-court and a minimum of 15 participants, with each squad having the ability to easily and quickly substitute others into the drill. Three different coaches could actually each be assigned to one of the three squads, with all three coaches having different points of emphasis to constantly observe and critique for their particular squad.

The primary emphasis of the drill is devoted to Squad A. Therefore, that group would have the largest number of points of emphasis. While points of emphasis certainly can come from the imagination of the coaching staff, some of the most important include the following:

- Make sure the tailback, halfback, and three fullbacks get in the proper positions after the offense has shot the ball (the tailback is called safety, the halfback is the designated half-rebounder/half-safety, and the three fullbacks are offensive rebounders).

- Ensure that all five players sprint back in their defensive fast break lanes (while looking over their inside shoulder) and set up defensively in the lane before building the defense from the inside out.

- Make sure that either the tailback or halfback becomes the ball man (TB in Diagram 7.47) while the other becomes the basket man (HB in Diagram 7.47).

- Ensure that the ball man and basket man use the proper procedures and techniques to defend the basket and buy their three defensive teammates some time in getting back.

- Make sure that all five players get out quickly and run the proper lanes while offensively executing their own primary and secondary fast breaks before moving into their half-court offenses.

Squad B's main points of emphasis should include use of the proper techniques and concepts in their half-court defensive philosophies. Squad C should focus on all the concepts, philosophies, and techniques used in their offensive fast break system—both the primary and secondary—as well as in their half court offense.

The Three-on-Two to Two-on-One Transition Drill

This drill can be a breakdown drill for specific players to work on their individual transition responsibilities and assignments, and can be set up primarily for the two most important players in a team's defensive transition. Remember that all players should work on these two defensive positions, because any player can end up in one of those particular roles. On all missed shots, there must be a tailback and also a halfback, illustrated in Diagram 7.48 as X1 and X2. While not disregarding the other players, the

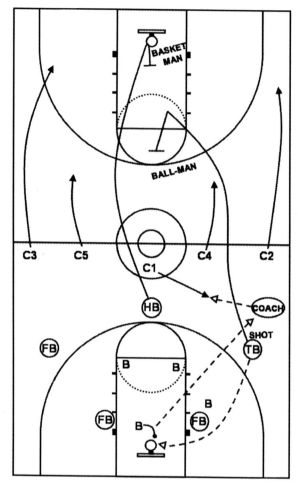

Diagram 7.47

two players that should be the main focal points of the coaching staff's attention are those that will become the first two defenders getting back via an offensive-to-defensive transition. They are called the basket man and the ball man.

If an offensive team shoots, misses, and surrenders a defensive rebound, two positions are assigned for the first two defenders who are to get back on defense. If the offensive team loses possession of the ball via a turnover, no definite defensive transitions are assigned. Instead, it is imperative that the offensive team's basket is immediately protected, regardless of what players get back first. Anyone could become the basket man and the ball man, which is why every player should practice these techniques and skills.

As in the majority of your drills, try to make this drill as game-realistic, competitive, and time-efficient as possible. With those goals in mind, incorporate some offensive concepts and philosophies for one group of players to work on as another group works on developing specific defensive skills.

The Three-on-Two Portion of the Drill

The drill can be set up with two defensive players (X1 and X2), literally sitting near the offense's sideline hash mark, and three offensive players (O1, O2, and O3) in lines that start on the offense's baseline. The ball is advanced via dribbling and/or passing with the three offensive players moving within their wide lanes as quickly as possible to attack their basket. The two defenders must quickly scramble to their feet and then sprint back to defend their basket. The first defender to actually get back should run

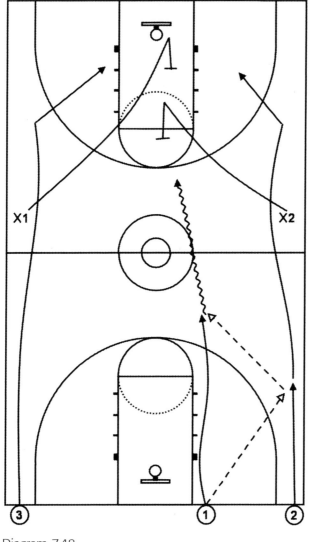

Diagram 7.48

to the middle of the free-throw lane and call, "Basket!" while the second defender to get back should call, "Ball!" thereby designating roles as the basket man and ball man (Diagram 7.48).

Another method of starting the drill is with the three offensive players (O1, O2, and O3) starting in a three-on-three defensive alignment against three other players (X3, X4, and X5), with the original two (potential) defenders (X1 and X2) making one or two passes before they shoot and miss to cause a defensive rebound. The original three defenders (soon to become offensive players O1, O2, and O3) work on boxing out, securing the rebound, and running a three-man fast break in the three lanes. The two original offensive players (X1 and X2) sprint back as quickly as possible, communicating loudly regarding who is to become ball man and basket man. The dummy offensive players (X3, X4, and X5) step off the court and get ready to step into the roles that O1, O2, and O3 are currently playing.

The first defender (X2 in Diagram 7.49) settles in near the dotted circle in the middle of the lane and yells, "Basket!" The second defender that gets back (X1 in Diagram 7.41) settles in the lane and approaches the dribbler as far out as the top of the key and yells, "Ball!" The ball man (X1) stops the dribble penetration of the dribbler, while the basket man (X2) protects the blocks and takes both the first and second perimeter passes. When the offensive team passes the ball to either wing, the basket man (X2) rotates out to defend the ball. As this is taking place, the original ball man (X1) drops quickly down the lane to protect the basket (Diagram 7.49).

The Two-on-One Portion of the Drill

When the three offensive players (O1, O2, and O3) lose possession of the ball via a made or missed shot or a turnover, either the shooter or the player who committed the turnover must turn and sprint back to protect the far basket by himself. The original two defenders (X1 and X2) would then sprint back and run a two-man offensive fast break against the new lone defender.

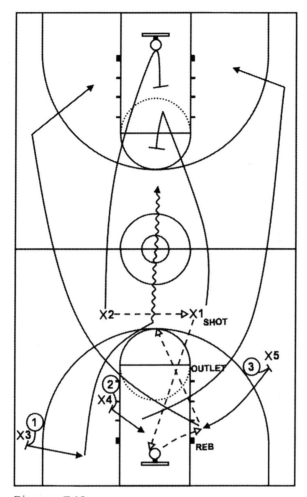

Diagram 7.49

8

The Corners Trap Offense

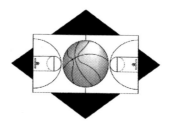

Introduction to the Corners Trap Offense

The trap offense is the only offense in this book that is not the typical half-court zone offense. This offense serves mostly as a half-court offense against various half-court trap defenses, but it is also very effective as a last-second shot offense at the end of a quarter, a semi-delay offense, or a complete delay game offense. It actually can be expanded to a three-quarter or full-court zone press offense once the ball is inbounded.

The basic alignment, the placement of personnel, and the rules and concepts are all the same whether corners is used against full-court, three-quarter court, or half-court pressure-type defenses. Once these are learned, understood, and practiced, the offense becomes an attack that can successfully be used against three different levels of zone trap pressures.

Corners is especially effective against odd front half-court trap defenses, such as the 1-3-1 or 1-2-2 trap defenses because the offensive players are spaced in a wider area than usual and are already in the natural gaps of the half-court defense. This approach attacks the actual alignment of the defense (#3, #4, #10).

Like all organized offenses, this offense still requires that all five of the offensive players be in the proper offensive locations (called spot-ups) and must follow the specific rules for each type of pass that can be made in this half-court trap offense. Multiple options that help prevent the offense from being predictable and scoutable by opposing teams is a major component of this offense (#2). This offense not only attacks the trap defense's weaknesses, but also counters the trap defense's main strength—the defense's aggressive nature (#3).

To attack half court traps, an offense should spread the defense out and try to fatigue it before frustrating the defense with eventual scores. Maintaining possession of the ball not only fatigues the defense, but it also prevents the opposition from being able to execute their own offense, and therefore, limiting their scoring opportunities (#26).

A team's overall offensive scheme could possibly have multiple secondary fast breaks in its transition game, with the one basic requirement of each secondary fast break being able to flow directly into the trap offense continuity (#1). If the secondary fast break does not produce transition points, every one of the secondary breaks utilized must end up in the same five offensive spot-ups that the trap offense continuity requires. This positioning gives the offense an immediate transition from the primary fast break (or a full-court press offense) into the secondary fast break and then into the half-court offense.

Corners trap offense will have several entries before entering into the continuity of the corners trap offense. The initial alignment with the wide spacing makes the alignment against half-court trap defenses a very effective (and a potential quick-hitting) offense (#4, #10).

Although few in number, these entries can be run out of multiple sets. Each set could also have the potential for a different repertoire of various quick-hitting entries (#2). If these quick-hitters do not produce immediate scores, the five players will end up in the spot-ups that are conducive for the trap offense to continue without resetting.

The five spot-up positions of this trap offense help allow for maximum offensive rebounding effectiveness. With the pressure defense chasing and trying to trap the ball, defensive box-outs and defensive rebounding is very difficult for the opposition to execute successfully. Therefore, offensive rebounding is a much more viable way for the offense to score. Offensive rebounding is a vital phase of any entire zone offensive scheme and can be a major source of a team's scoring (#4, #8). One important offensive concept is to overload the weakside rebounding area of the defense so that the offense can gain a numerical personnel advantage on the defense. Each offensive player in the corners trap offense has clearly spelled out offensive rebounding assignments and responsibilities.

One important key of the corners trap offense is to minimize the amount of defensive pressure that will be applied by the opposition to the offensive personnel.

The locations of the trap offense's spot-ups are strategically spread out (both vertically and horizontally) so that the trap defense has a maximum amount of territory to cover, causing the opposition's trappers to also be spread out. Spreading the defense ultimately thins and weakens the defense and corners are then ready to attack the weaknesses (#4, #10).

Passing and reversing the ball from the wider locations and positions of the players causes the trapping defenders to have to chase the ball, which makes it difficult for the defense to keep up with the ball and very difficult to maintain pressure on the ball. Skip passes can be very effective against half-court, three-quarter court, or full-court pressure and trapping defenses (#9, #10, #15).

Placement of Personnel

Using the standard offensive personnel numbering system, O1 should be the point guard (and should be the best ball handler and interior passer), O2 should be the big guard, O3 is the small forward, O4 is the power forward that acts more like a small forward, and O5 is the center. Both O2 and O3 should be very good ball handlers as well as good perimeter shooters. O4, O5, and possibly O2 should be good post players and offensive rebounders, but should also be able to handle, catch, and pass the basketball (especially against double-team traps).

It is of paramount importance that all five of the players in the corners trap offense be able to handle the basketball—probably more so than in any other offense. If this offense is being used, the opposition has stepped up its defensive pressure by using some type of a trap defense at a level anywhere from half-court to the full-court level.

Offensive players must realize how important the basketball is to trapping defenders. Defenders in a pressure-type defense have their whole focus on the basketball and offensive players must take advantage of that by making realistic ball fakes and shot fakes (#14). Offensive players should also attack the trapping defense by disappearing from the trapping defense behind the defenders before making cuts to get open. What the trapping defenders cannot see, they cannot defend (#16, #22).

Every player must be able to dribble and pass the ball against double-team pressure to get open, to catch the ball, and to act in an aggressive and attacking manner against the pressure-type of defense (but still remain under control). Each player must be able to shot fake, ball fake, catch the basketball and become an immediate threat to the trapping defense, and defeat the aggressive nature of the defenders (#11, #12, #13, #14). Specific cuts after passes to the interior can be especially effective against half-court traps (#20, #21, #22).

It is also important that the four perimeter players (O1, O2, O3, and O4) be effective perimeter shooters, particularly off of the pass. This skill will help the offense to vertically and horizontally stretch the defense so that the offense can then attack the inside of the trap defense. It is also very important that all four of the perimeter players know the various types of zone dribbles and passes and how to use them effectively at the appropriate times (#12, #15).

The players that end up in the middle of the trap offense (most likely O5 or O4 and sometimes O2) must be able to catch the various types of passes made to them on the interior and also have a variety of post moves to be able to effectively score inside (#20, #21, #22, #23, #24, #25). The offense has much more effectiveness if O5, O4, O3, and O2 can interchange their respective positions. All must be able to read the defense, particularly trappers and the interior defense.

Every offensive player must have an attitude of expecting to defeat the pressure defense, not to just survive it. This attitude will make the offensive players more aggressive and focused, both of which are necessary for the offense to succeed. Offensive techniques and skills are very important, but the overall attitude of every player is of equal importance to the overall success of the offense.

Spot-up Locations and Descriptions

The spot-ups for the corners trap offense continuity are somewhat different than the spot-ups of zone offenses previously described. A major reason is that this offense is not a typical zone offense, but an offense that should be utilized against half-court defensive traps (instead of typical zone defenses). Because of the aggressiveness of half-court trap defenses, the spot-up locations of the corners trap offense are much wider apart than the typical half-court zone offenses.

The basic spot-up positions are defined with the location of the ball dictating that side of the court as being the ballside, with the opposite side being called the weakside or the offside. These spot-ups are set up in an even front alignment—having a ballside wing, a weakside wing, a ballside post, a ballside corner, and a weakside corner. Both the ballside wing and the weakside wing are located slightly higher than the free-throw line extended, just outside the three-point line, on both sides of the court. These two spots can be called wide-elbow areas (area A in Diagram 8.1). The ballside post position is always on the ballside, somewhere from the first notch above the low-post block (area B in Diagram 8.1) up to the intersection of the free-throw line and lane line (otherwise known as the tight-elbow area, which is illustrated as area C in Diagram 8.1). The ballside corner position is always on the ballside, a step off the baseline, midway between the lane and the sideline (area D in Diagram 8.1). The weakside corner position for this particular trap offense is located on the first notch above the block on the weakside (in area E in Diagram 8.1).

Diagram 8.2 shows the five spot-up positions for the corners trap offense when the ball is on the right side of the floor, with BC representing the ballside corner, BP the ballside post, WC the weakside corner, BW the ballside wing, and WW the weakside wing.

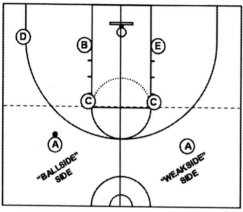

Diagram 8.1

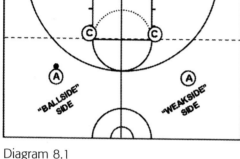

Diagram 8.2

Quick Options

Diagram 8.3 illustrates the initial passing options from the stationary spot-up positions. O1 can pass to O2 (B), O5 (D), or O3 (A). A pass to O2 (B) allows O2 to pass inside to O5 (D), back to O1 (C), or skip pass to O3 (#15, #20). Anyone receiving the pass has the opportunities to shoot, drive, or make an additional pass to a teammate (#13).

Diagram 8.4 exhibits the continued use of the skip pass. O2 and O3 skip pass back and forth, while O5 tries to seal his defender off for a quick pass inside (#15, #20, #21, #22, #23, #24, #25).

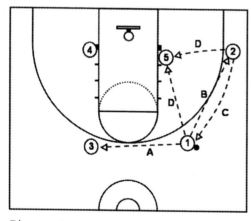

Diagram 8.3

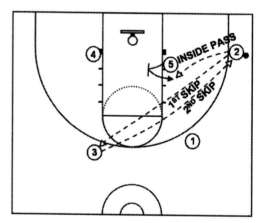

Diagram 8.4

Seal moves are when a ballside post (O5) sees the skip pass go over his head from the original passer (O2) to the weakside wing (O3), and then seals off the post defender, (XC) who is either half or three-quarter fronting him on the original ballside. The post player (O5) then looks for an inside pass from the new passer (O3) (Diagram 8.5) (#15, #23, #24).

Diagram 8.6 shows the ball being reversed around the perimeter and O4 and O5 running the basic continuity of the corners continuity (just spread so it will attack a trap instead of a standard zone defense) (#9, #10). O4 steps out to the deep corner. O5 chases the ball to the new ballside post area and O2 starts to step into the new weakside low-post area.

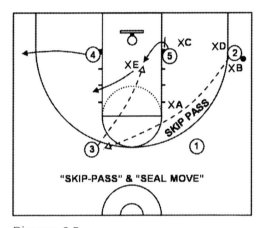

Diagram 8.5

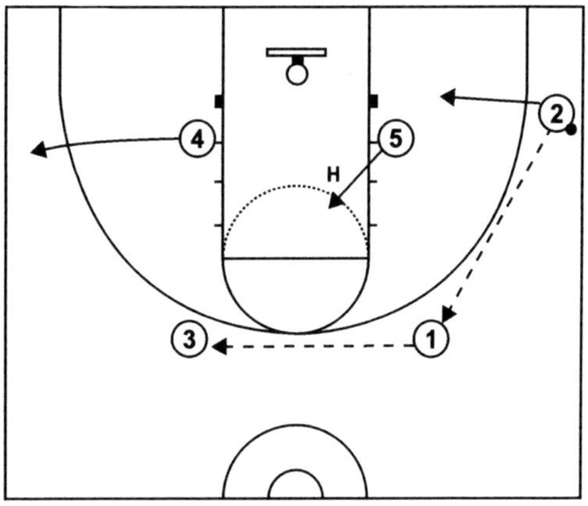

Diagram 8.6

It is often dangerous to keep the ball on one side of the court against a trapping defense, but sometimes the attacking team has no other recourse. When this instance occurs, it is best to have the opposite post player cut to the open area at the high post (Diagram 8.7). A pass inside to O4 will get a look inside to O5, who should have position on his defender for a lay-up (#4, #20, #24).

Pin-screens are screens off of the ball to attempt to screen a zone defender and pin him in for an offensive shooter to be freed up for a perimeter shot. In the corners trap offense, this shot can only take place after the second skip pass is made. Diagram 8.8 shows an example of O2 first making a skip pass to O3 and then receiving a skip pass from O3, with O5 pin-screening for him. After the pin-screen, O5 may again seal off and post-up the zone defender in the new ballside post area. On the second skip pass, O2 could look to shoot, to make an inside pass on the seal-off by O5, or possibly to even skip pass back to O3 (#13, #15, #18, #24).

A back-out dribble is the dribble at the end of a gap dribble, where the dribbler (O1) backs out of the defensive trap that he has purposely dribbled into. The back-out dribble is to protect the dribbler and the ball after he has lured two defenders to guard him, thus giving the offense a numerical advantage of four off-the-ball players against the three remaining defenders (Diagram 8.9) (#4, #12). The back-out dribble is exceptionally effective against double team defenders who will continue to chase the dribbler until they can set the trap. This move stretches the defense and can actually distort the defense, thus weakening it (#3).

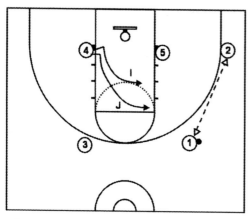

Diagram 8.7   Diagram 8.8

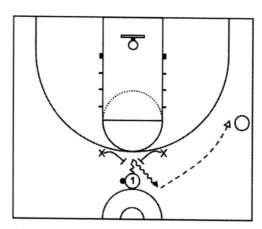

Diagram 8.9

Offense's Continuity Rules

Diagram 8.10 displays the corner continuity, given briefly in Chapter 2. It can be used against basic zones as well as trapping zones. Hence, if you are facing a team that alternates the use of the zone as well as trap out the zone, you can run the corner continuity without having to recognize which defense you are facing.

O1 passes to O3 (Diagram 8.10) (#9, #17). This pass keys O4 to cut into the corner, O5 to cut behind the zone defenders into a gap in the interior of the zone trap before ending up at the new ballside low post, and O2 to cut along the baseline to the new weakside low post (#9, #10, #16, #17, #20, #21, #22). The attack now has changed sides of the court, hence the continuity.

To protect the interior of the trap defense, oftentimes a defense will bring in extra defenders from the perimeter area to help their interior defenders. This play will strengthen the interior of the zone defense, but will weaken the perimeter of the zone. This weakness must be taken advantage of swiftly and easily by simply making one or two skip passes from the ballside to the weakside. This defensive technique should help free up the weakside perimeter player. O2 skip passes the ball crosscourt to the weakside teammate, O3, who should have his feet and hands ready to catch the ball and quickly shoot (from the perimeter) (Diagram 8.11) (#3, #9, #13, #15, #17).

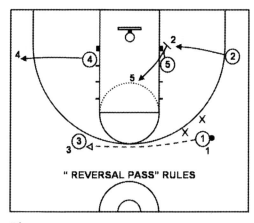

" REVERSAL PASS" RULES

Diagram 8.10

" SKIP PASS" RULES

Diagram 8.11

O3 receives the skip pass and can make inside passes to teammates running the continuity, take three-point shots on the perimeter, or make another skip pass back to the original side. When the ball is swung quickly from one side of the court to the other, it gives inside players great opportunities to establish position advantages over defenders, and it is inside players' jobs to then maintain those position advantages and attack the defense with fundamentally sound post moves (#3, #9, #13, #15, #17, #22, #23, #24).

Two types of skip passes could be used in the corners trap offense. Diagram 8.11 illustrates the skip pass from the ballside corner (O2) to the weakside wing (O3), and Diagram 8.12 shows that the other type could originate from the ballside wing (O1) to the weakside corner (O4) for a quick inside shot opportunity. Both are invaluable to the corners trap offense and must be performed correctly and frequently for the offense to be effective (#9, #15, #17).

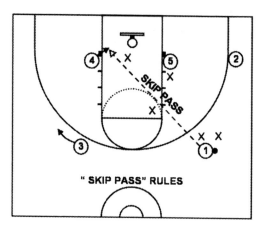

Diagram 8.12

The skip pass should be used often against a zone trap team that sinks the perimeter players to prevent inside passes and shots. The most frequent opening is the post player who breaks behind the zone into a gap high or midpost region (#3, #15, #16, #22). In Diagram 8.11, the pass from O2 to O3 and the cut by O5 should allow O3 to pass to O5 who immediately looks opposite to O2 for the lay-up (#20). This move occurs often against trapping zones. Also, if the defenders race to cover this pass inside to O5, then O2 is often open for the lob pass from O3 (Diagram 8.11) (#23).

Diagram 8.12 illustrates O1 making the skip pass to O4 on the weakside low-post area because the defense is over-protecting the ballside options—the ballside block (O5) and the perimeter threat on the ballside (O2) (#3). Diagrams 8.13 through 8.16 shows the defensive traps being set as the ball is passed to one corner (O2) from the ballside wing (O1) (#9). O1 could reverse to O3, but the skip pass from O2 to O3 allows a quicker reversal (#15). These four diagrams also show the openings in the middle as the ball is reversed. Diagram 8.16 illustrates the pass to O5 and the ensuing

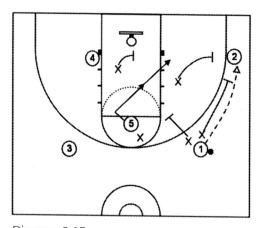

Diagram 8.13

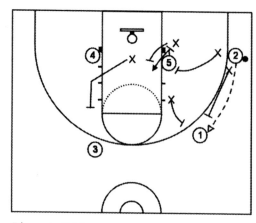

Diagram 8.14

dump down to O2 (#13, #16, #20, #21). The trapping defense, no matter its slides, cannot recover to stop this lay-up (#3, #4). Ball fakes will compel the trap to move in one direction and the actual pass in the other direction is frequently open (#14).

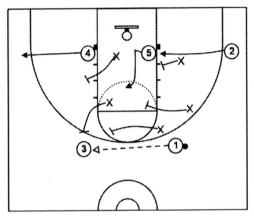

Diagram 8.15

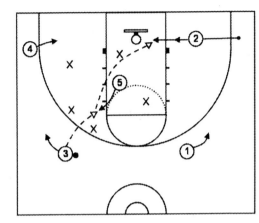

Diagram 8.16

Options and Special Rules

When the ballside wing (O1) has possession of the ball and he makes the down pass to the corner (O2), the post player in the center of the offense (O5) should slide down to the new ballside low-post area (#17, #22). As this move takes place, the weakside corner (O4) can gap cut across the lane and settle in anywhere in the tight elbow area on the ballside high post (Diagram 8.17) (#4, #22).

After gap-cutting to the high-post area and not receiving a pass from either O1 or O2, this flasher (O4) could either empty out or return to his original location at his own discretion (Diagram 8.18). Another possibility is that he could slide down to the ballside

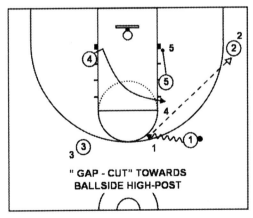

Diagram 8.17

low-post area, push out the original ballside post (O5), and make that player the new weakside corner on the opposite side of the floor (Diagram 8.19).

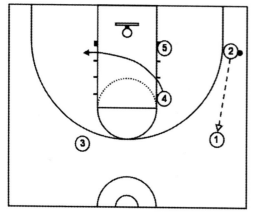

Diagram 8.18

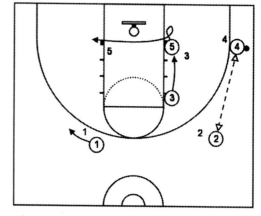

Diagram 8.19

If the ball is reversed via a skip pass or a reversal pass while the offense has two post players in the overload option, the two post players could make x-cuts as both players make gap cuts, and chase the ball across the free-throw lane to the opposite side of the court (#9, #17, #22). Diagram 8.20 illustrates the overload option of the corners trap offense being used first on the left side of the court before a reversal pass is made from O1 to O2. O5 at the low post and O4 at the high post make x-cuts across the lane and, after momentarily posting up, O4 ends up stepping out to the new ballside corner. O5 then fills in and posts up at the new ballside low-post area (#4, #10, #13, #14, #16, #17, #19, #20, #21, #22, #23, #24, #25). This maneuver places all five players back in the corner spot-up positions so that this continuity offense can continue attacking the defense (#26).

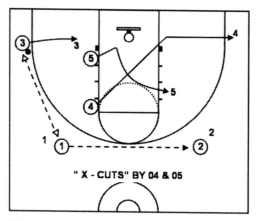

Diagram 8.20

Offensive Rebounding and Transition Responsibilities

Diagram 8.21 illustrates the typical rebounding responsibilities and defensive transition duties. They are the same as has been described previously on each of the zone attacks.

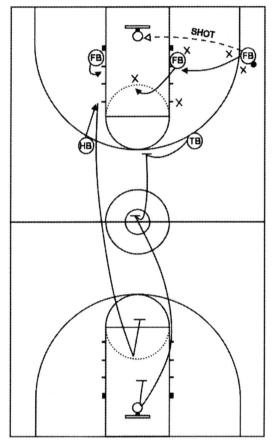

Diagram 8.21

Primary Fast Break into the Secondary Fast Break into the Continuity Offense

The same fast break and secondary fast break, described in Chapter 2, is the first phase of the attack. The second phase is the corner trap continuity, which can be run from spot-up positions, from quick hitting entries, or from the continuity itself. When the shot is taken, the transition responsibilities and the rebounding duties begin.

Entries into the Trap Offense

Entries or plays can be defined as quick-hitters that attempt to score with various offensive actions and a matter of just one or two passes. Each entry is designed to make sure that all five offensive players will end up in specific spot-up positions, if and when the entry fails in its attempt to score. The trap's entries are the initial attack on the opposition's defense, but the continuity maintains the constant threat to the opposition's trap defense. Specific entries can be developed to attack general weaknesses of specific trap defenses, as well as highlight and take advantage of individual's offensive strengths, or possibly opposing individual's defensive weaknesses (#3, #4, #5, #6).

The Lines Alignment/Set Entries

The lines set is a zone trap offensive set that has a variety of entries that can be run out of this set. Other entries can be designed to attack specific weaknesses of the trap defense or weaknesses of individual opponents. One of the two entries that can flow into corners trap offense can be called *lines to big to corners* or *lines to small to corners*. The lines set is most effective when running against a 1-3-1 trap defense, even though it can be run against a 1-2-1-1 or a 1-2-2 trap.

The lines set is an alignment that starts one post player on the right block (O4) and the other post player on the left elbow (O5). The offense has a wing player (O2) located in the right deep corner and the other player (O3) at the wing area on the left side, with the point guard (O1) centered up at the top of the key. After the entry has been executed and no shot or turnover takes place, the lines set will have all five players in the corners trap offense continuity spot-ups. With the ball on the right wing, this action places offensive player O1 at the ballside wing, O5 at the weakside wing, O4 at the ballside post, O2 at the ballside corner, and O3 at the weakside post (Diagram 8.22).

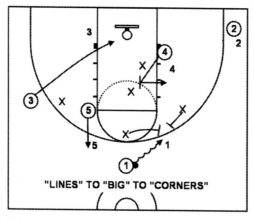

"LINES" TO "BIG" TO "CORNERS"

Diagram 8.22

Two entries that can be executed out of the lines set are described in the sections that follow. These two entries are called big and small. This play is initiated by O1 making a combination of a gap dribble and a freeze dribble dribbling at the outside shoulder of the wing defender.

The point could initiate this dribble toward the defensive wing on either side. This example is when the point dribbles toward the low-line side, which is the right side in Diagram 8.22. O4 makes a duck-in cut, while O2 stays in the deep corner and prepares himself to receive the pass and quickly make one of the three choices he has when he does receive the ball from the point: to shoot, drive to the basket, or pass to an open teammate (#13).

One of the designated weakside players (O3 or O5) makes a cut by stepping out to the weakside elbow area, while the other weakside player (O5 or O3) makes a dive-cut to the basket. The big entry heading to the right side designates that the big weakside player on the left side (O5) steps outside the three-point line, while the other weakside player on the left side (O3) makes the dive cut to the basket. The point (O1) dribbles to the right into the potential defensive trap, while reading the post player (O4) that is making a duck-in cut and also reading the actual weakside wing defender. If that specific weakside defender stays high, O1 looks to hit the teammate who is making the dive-cut to the basket (O3 on the big call). Instead, if that same defender sags off low to protect the basket, O1 should look to hit the teammate who has stepped out to the weakside elbow area (O5 on the big call). A short and simple phrase used to teach the point guard his reads on the weakside of the 1-3-1 trap defense is the following: "If the weakside defender goes low, look to throw high. If the defender goes high, look to throw low." One of the weakside players must be open with the way this particular defense is played. The specific strength of this entry/play is attacking the specific weakness of this particular 1-3-1 trap defense—the weakside slide.

If no inside pass is made by O1, all five of the players are in the proper spot-ups so that the corners trap offense can easily continue for an indefinite period of time. Diagram 8.22 gives an illustration of the big entry out of the lines set with the ball being dribbled toward the right side. The big entry dribbled toward the left side (the high-line side) is illustrated in Diagram 8.23, with all five of the players again spotting up in the correct positions when no shot or turnover takes place.

The big entry is much more effective when run toward the right side (low line side), even though it may be run toward the high-line side of the floor. The problem with the entry starting towards the left side (Diagram 8.23) is that some perimeter players are out of position, as well as missing out on the post player combination that is normally the most effective. When big is run to the left side (Diagram 8.23), O4 ends up as a perimeter player at the weakside wing and O2 at the weakside corner area. O3 flare-cuts to the new ballside deep corner position and O5 becomes the current ballside post player, with O1 (always) being the ballside wing. Minor adjustments could be utilized to place all five of the players in the proper spot-up positions.

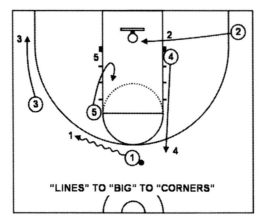

"LINES" TO "BIG" TO "CORNERS"

Diagram 8.23

Diagram 8.24 illustrates the lines to small to corners offensive scheme with O1 dribbling to the right side (O4), toward the low line and away from the high line. The post player on the right side posts up by ducking into the free-throw lane while O2 remains in the deep corner. The new weakside post player (O5) dives toward the basket, while the weakside perimeter player on that side (O3) steps up to the weakside wing area (Diagram 8.24) (#12, #16, #17, #19, #20).

The small entry run to the left side of the floor is shown in Diagram 8.25. The small weakside player on the right side (O2) is the player that steps outside the three-point line while the remaining weakside player on the right side (O4) seals off the weakside wing defender and steps to the basket. The ballside post player on this high-line side (O5) must button hook into any open gap in the free-throw lane and post-up, while the ballside perimeter player (O3) must flare-cut to the ballside corner.

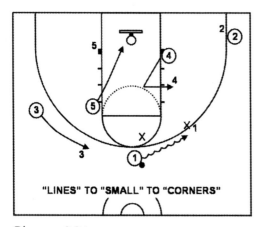

"LINES" TO "SMALL" TO "CORNERS"

Diagram 8.24

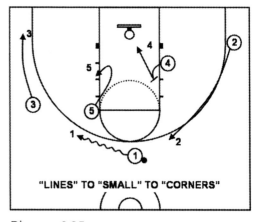

"LINES" TO "SMALL" TO "CORNERS"

Diagram 8.25

The Straight Alignment/Set Entries

The straight set is an offensive set that has two entries/plays that can be run out of this alignment. Again, both entries are designed to be quick-hitters that will either accent particular strengths of the offensive alignment or specific offensive individuals, or the entries could attempt to attack the specific weaknesses of the opposition's trap defense and/or certain weaknesses of individual opponents located in the trap defense (#3, #4, #6). The straight (big or small entry) to corners is the call made telling the players what alignment to initially set up in (straight), what entry to then run (big or small), and what continuity offense to end up in (corners). The straight set is best when running against a 1-3-1 trap defense or against a 1-2-2 trap defense.

The straight set is an alignment that has the post players aligned at each side at the tight elbow areas (O4 on the right high-post area and O5 on the left high-post area), with O2 on the right wing and O3 on the left wing. The two wings are lined up on each side of the free throw line extended, just outside of the three-point line, with the point guard (O1) centered up at the top of the key (Diagram 8.26) (#10).

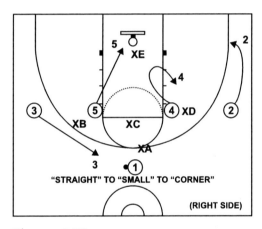

Diagram 8.26

If the straight to small to corners entry has O1 dribbling to the right side, the weakside wing (in this case it is O3) steps out to the weakside wing area while the weakside post player (O5 in Diagram 8.26) dives to the basket. The ballside wing (O2) makes a flare cut to the deep corner on the new ballside, while the new ballside post (O4) ducks in to the middle of the lane from the high-post area before posting up in the ballside low-post area. If the entry is executed without a shot or turnover, all five of the players end up in the corners trap offense continuity spot-ups (#26).

The same two entries (the big and small entries) that can be run out of the lines set can also be run out of the straight set and are described in the sections that follow. Each of the entries will end up in the spot-up positions of the corners trap offense, which again allows the offense to continually attack the opposition's defense. Both entries can be run to the left side as well as the right side, even though some minor adjustments must be made to get the proper people in the correct spot-up positions. Every coaching staff can create other entries to be run out of the straight set that will fit their team's specific personnel.

Each entry to either side is started by O1 dribbling into the gap between the defensive point and the wing defender on that particular side of the floor (#12). The point could initiate this dribble toward the wide elbow area on the either side. Diagram 8.26 shows that this dribble should draw both the defensive point (XA) and the ballside wing defender (XD) on the dribbler, leaving three remaining defenders (XB, XC, and XE) to cover the remaining four offensive players.

Diagram 8.26 also illustrates the example of the small entry being run out of the straight set on the right side. O4 gets open in any vacuum or gap in the middle of the lane before he ends up posting up on the (newly-declared) ballside post. O2 makes a flare cut toward the deep-corner area and prepares to receive the pass from O1. O2 should quickly make one of the many choices he has when he does receive the ball from the point (as he does in the same entry in the lines set). His choices are to either quickly shoot off of the pass, to make an inside pass to O4, or to make a skip pass to O3, besides having the option of making an up pass back up to O1. The small entry designates that the small weakside player on the left side (O3) is the player that steps outside the three-point line near the wide-elbow area, while the other weakside player on the left side (O5) makes the dive cut to the basket. The point (O1) dribbles into the potential trap, while reading the teammate that is making a duck-in cut (O4 in this case) and also reading the actual defender on the (new) weakside of the defense (XB). The points of emphasis of the point guard are the same for the small entry out of the straight set as for small entry out of the lines set. If that specific weakside defender (XB) stays high, O1 looks to hit the teammate (O5) who is making the low dive-cut to the basket. If that same defender (XB) goes low to protect the basket, O1 should look to hit the teammate who has stepped out high to the weakside elbow area (O3).

The same simple phrase that is used to teach the point guard on the reads on the weakside of the 1-3-1 trap defense still comes into play in this particular offensive set. If the weakside wing defender goes low, look to throw high. If that wing defender goes high, look to throw low. One of the weakside offensive players must be open because of the way this particular trap defense is executed. This action again capitalizes on the specific weakness of this particular 1-3-1 trap defense. If no inside pass is made by O1 to the ballside post (O4), all five of the players result in the proper spot-ups so that the corners trap offense can be easily run indefinitely.

Diagram 8.27 gives an illustration of the big entry out of the straight set with the ball being dribbled toward the right side. If no shots are taken, minor adjustments must be utilized to place all five of the players in the proper spot-up positions. On the ball reversal pass to O5 (the post player who has ended up on the weakside wing area), if nothing develops from the pass, that player must somehow end up in the ballside post position. This alignment will place the proper personnel in their appropriate positions for the offense to operate at maximum efficiency. This play can be done by O5 making a down pass to O3 and making a hard cut to become the (new) ballside post, O4 becoming the weakside corner, with O1 and O2 rotating over to the two wing positions on top of the corners trap offense (Diagram 8.28).

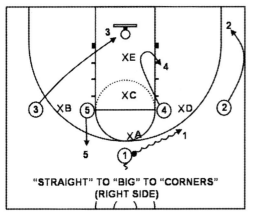

"STRAIGHT" TO "BIG" TO "CORNERS"
(RIGHT SIDE)

Diagram 8.27

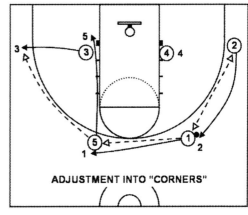

ADJUSTMENT INTO "CORNERS"

Diagram 8.28

The small entry (out of the straight set) is shown with the point guard dribbling into the trap on the left side of the floor and O3 flaring just outside the three-point line on the baseline of the zone trap. The post player on the left side (O5) makes the same button hook cut to post-up in the (new) ballside post area. The weakside players now on the right side make the appropriate cuts on the weakside. With the small entry, the smaller weakside player (O2 in this case) is the player that steps out beyond the three-point line in the wide weakside elbow area and the weakside bigger player is the player (O4) that makes the dive cut to the basket. When this straight alignment and this small entry are run to this side of the floor, no adjustments of personnel have to be made since all five of the offensive players are already in the proper locations to be able to run corners trap offense continuously (Diagrams 8.29 and 8.30) (#12, #16, #19, #22).

Diagrams 8.29 and 8.30 illustrate the small entry being run toward the left side of the court. The difference in executing the small entry (out of the same straight set/alignment) toward the left side and the right side is essentially that O2 and O3 switch assignments and spot-up locations at the ballside corner and the weakside wing.

The Spread Alignment/Set Entries

The spread alignment/set is an alignment that should be used against more aggressive types of half-court trap defenses that attempt to deny the offensive point guard from

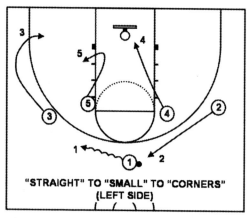

"STRAIGHT" TO "SMALL" TO "CORNERS"
(LEFT SIDE)

Diagram 8.29

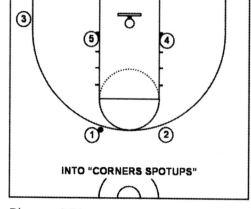

INTO "CORNERS SPOTUPS"

Diagram 8.30

dribbling the ball across the 10-second timeline. It is better if used against odd front trap defenses, such as a 1-3-1, 1-2-1-1, or a 1-2-2 half-court trap defense.

The initial positions of the spread alignment/set are two guard positions (O3 on the left and O1 on the right) so that they are one or two steps outside the imaginary vertical lines of the free-throw lane extended toward the timeline. The two forward positions are lined up at the free-throw lines extended and about two feet from each sideline (with O4 on the left and O2 on the right side) and one post player who should line up on the second notch above the block on either side of the floor (Diagram 8.31). If either entry is to be executed out of this alignment, the point guard (O1) can simply call out spread (alignment name), *big* or *small* (entry name), or *corners* (continuity name).

The main points of emphasis in attacking any type of aggressive defensive pressure is to always have the dribbling point guard quickly dribble the ball up to the timeline, but

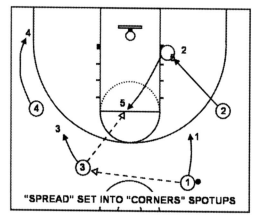

"SPREAD" SET INTO "CORNERS" SPOTUPS

Diagram 8.31

then read and gauge the degree of defensive pressure that is about to be placed on him. When having a teammate with him in the backcourt, both players should be spaced apart from each other and appropriately spaced from their respective sidelines. The teammate in the backcourt without the ball (O3 in Diagram 8.31) should always stay behind the level of the ball. This concept allows the offense a safe outlet, so that the ball can most likely be reversed when other passing lanes in the frontcourt are closed.

A half-court trap offense should always have at least one player in the frontcourt (O5) to be an immediate threat to the defense for a quick score. Coaches should constantly emphasize to his players that the overall offensive philosophy against any type of defense (be it full-court or half-court) is that the offense should not want to just survive the defense, but should want to soundly defeat the opposition's defense.

The nearest ballside player in the frontcourt (O2 when O1 has the ball and O4 when O3 has the ball) should be ready to widen out and/or step up to help relieve any defensive denial pressure. It is best for the dribbler that is approaching the 10-second timeline (O1 or O3) to reverse the ball at least one time before the ball can be actually dribbled across the timeline. Coaches should use the phrase, "The initial dribbler that is bringing the ball up-court should not be the dribbler that crosses the timeline." This technique of dribbling the ball up and teasing the defense before then reversing the ball and finally dribbling or passing the ball across the timeline can really take a lot of the hustle and the overall aggressiveness out of the trapping defense.

Ball fakes against any types of zone defenses, full-court presses, or half-court trap defenses anywhere on the court followed by reversal passes (particularly in the backcourt) can really take the sting out of pressure defenses, since the trapping defenses must react quickly to the basketball (#14). Ball fakes cause the defense to react and move more often and can wear down defenders.

Because of the extra added pressure that some half-court trap defenses place upon offenses, the spread alignment/set is one set that does not actually have entries/plays to utilize before getting into the corners trap offense continuity. Instead, a couple of rules that applied after particular passes are made. One of the rules is that if either guard—O1 or O3 (O1 in this illustration)—reverses the ball to the opposite guard in the frontcourt (O3 in Diagram 8.31), the lone post player (O5) should flash (from behind the defense) through the heart of the zone trap to the center of the free-throw line (or possibly higher if defensive pressure causes him to do so) (#16, #20).

The weakside forward becomes O2 (when O1 reverses to O3 on the opposite side from O2), and on the reversal pass, he makes a dive cut to the basket (#10, #22). At the same time, O4 makes a flare cut to the deep ballside corner, while O5 is in the middle of the defense, and the two guards maintain proper spacing on top of the offense. This alignment places all five of the players in the proper spot-ups to start (and also continue into) the corners trap offense (Diagram 8.31).

Whenever the ball is passed to the post player (O5) after he has flashed to the middle of the free-throw line, the extend-the-pass concept is applied (#20, #21). In other words, if O3 passes the ball to O5, the weakside forward (O2) makes the dive cut to the weakside block area, while the ballside forward (O4) makes a flare cut to the deep corner. Both guards (O3 and O1) flare-cut slightly, but remain in the general vicinity close enough to be reliable receivers for O5 in the middle of the floor (Diagram 8.32).

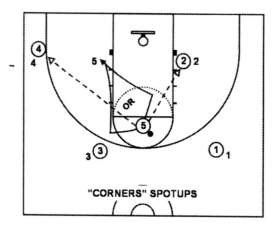

Diagram 8.32

If the pass is made to O4 in the deep corner from O3 or O5, the post player (O5) slides down and posts up in the new ballside low-post area. This action will result in good shots taken, or at least all five of the players in the proper spot-ups for the offense to be able to easily continue in the corners trap offense (#17, #26).

Anytime the ball reaches the ballside forward (O3) on the left side or O2 on the right side (in Diagram 8.33), the post player (O5) should make a dive cut or a gap-cut to that ballside post area (or should already be in that position), while the new weakside forward (O4 in Diagram 8.33) dive cuts to the weakside block area. The two guards (O1 and O3) remain out on top with the proper spacing between themselves and the basketball (Diagram 8.33). This action again puts everyone in the correct spot-ups for the corners trap offense to be executed indefinitely (#10, #26).

The last alignment that can be implemented is a set that not surprisingly is called the corners set. If the coaching staff wants to not only end up in corners but also start in this particular set, they simply call, "Corners to corners." The corners set is another alignment that can (and should) be used against more aggressive types of half-court trap defenses that attempt to deny the offensive point guard from dribbling the ball across the 10-second timeline. It is very effective against odd front trap defenses, such as a 1-3-1, a 1-2-1-1, or a 1-2-2 half-court trap defense.

The initial positions of the corners set are defined as two guard positions (O3 on the left and O1 on the right). The two guards should line up so that they again are one or two steps outside the imaginary vertical lines of the free-throw lane extended toward the timeline. The two forward positions (O4 on the left side and O2 on the right side) are lined up at deep along the baseline, with the ballside corner (O2) out wider toward the sideline and possibly up as far as the free-throw line extended (if defensive pressure warrants the move) (Diagram 8.34.) The weakside corner (O4 in this illustration) should be on or near the weakside block area, very close to the basket and behind the defense, making him a very dangerous weapon for the offense (#16).

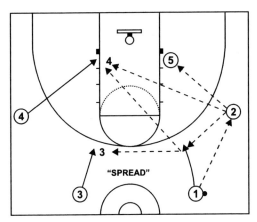

Diagram 8.33

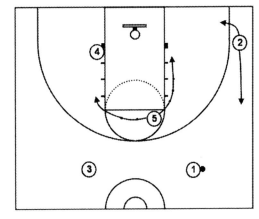

Diagram 8.34

Breakdown Drills for the Zone Offense

Shooting drills and movement drills have already been presented in Chapter 3 (spot-up shooting drills for the corner continuity) and in Chapter 7 (breakdown drills for all the zone offenses). In this section, we will concentrate only on drills to teach the movements involved in the corner trapping continuity. These drills can be used to teach and re-teach the timing of the cuts.

Diagrams 8.35, 8.36, and 8.37 reveal the entire continuity with all the possible passing and cutting options. Each drill should be looked at separately.

O3 passes to O2 who passes to O1 who passes to O4 (Diagram 8.35) (#10, #13, #14, #15, #16, #17, #19, #20, #21, #22, #23, #24, #25). O3 times his cut into the gap as O4 receives the pass. O4 immediately turns to find O3 breaking near the basket. If the pass is not available to O3 (#20, #22), O5 and O2 should have found gaps in the perimeter (#21).

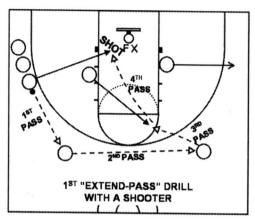

**1ST "EXTEND-PASS" DRILL
WITH A SHOOTER**

Diagram 8.35

Of course the drill can begin with O3 skip passing to O1 (Diagram 8.35) (#15). Or, O4 can be posting up while O3 is working to get the ball inside to him (#20, #24, #25). The most important thing being taught and re-taught is the timing of the passes and cuts. A by-product is the actual running and re-running of the entire continuity. If you wish to drill on any of the fundamentals, the 55-second shooting drills in Chapter 7 should be used.

Diagram 8.36 shows the entire reversal of the ball into the opposite corner (#10, #13, #14, #15, #16, #17). When the ball reaches the corner, O5, can pass inside to the cutting O4. O4 must find the opening in the zone defense (#20, #21, #22, #23, #24, #25).

Before you can fully understand these drills, you should review the concepts shown. For example, in the sentence above, #21 refers to, "on a pass to the middle, the perimeter players reposition themselves." In other words, on the pass to O4, the three perimeter players (O1, O2, and O5) find the gaps in the perimeter to receive a pass back outside. A pass from O4 to any of the three activates #13 and #14. A shot by any of the five players activates #8 and #9.

Diagram 8.37 illustrates the perimeter passing the ball back and forth while the inside three run the continuity. A skip pass can be used as well. This drill permits the inside three to read the passes and keep breaking in and out following the passes until a shot is finally taken. This drill can be used as a no shooting drill to accomplish, in only a few minutes, multiple gaps cuts. Also, the greatest benefit of no shooting would be O4 having to constantly check and re-check the opposite block when he receives the pass from the perimeter.

Diagrams 8.38 and 8.39 are two illustrations of how a coaching staff can place offensive passers and receivers, as well as defensive trappers and an interceptor, so that offensive players can work on dribbling in and out of traps (in addition to working on the technique of reading the defense to find the open teammate and ultimately passing out of the trap). Cutters/flashers, receivers, dribblers/passers, and defensive players in the drill can be placed in the various locations where the coaching staff feels improvement needs to be made.

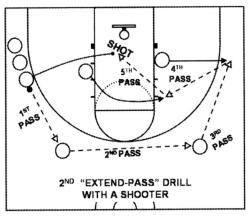

Diagram 8.36

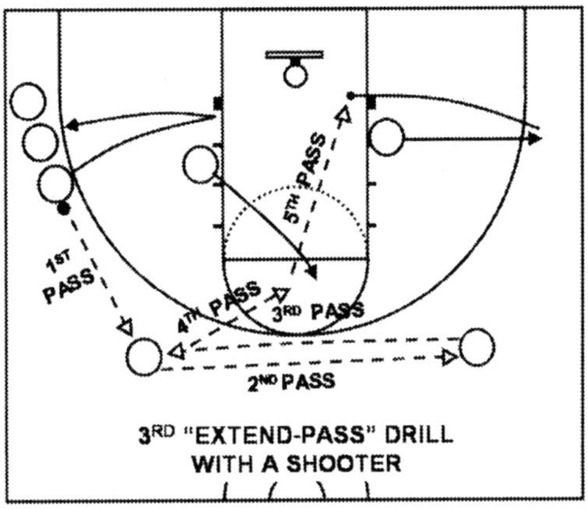

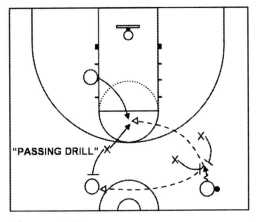

Diagram 8.37

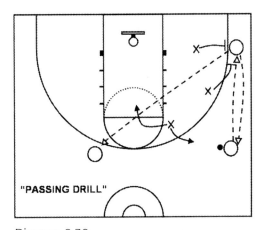

Diagram 8.38

Diagram 8.39

Conclusion

The corners trap offense can be a productive offense that incorporates sound philosophies and concepts and many of these concepts can capitalize on some of the trap defense's strengths and transform them into weaknesses. Responsibilities of every phase of the offensive game are clearly defined and assigned to specific players to make the offense carefully planned out. Doing so makes the corners trap offense efficient, productive, and successful.

The corners trap offense has the flexibility of being able to use different alignments/sets to make this offense adaptable to attack various types of trap defenses that have even or odd fronts (i.e., 2-1-2 zones, 2-3 zones, 1-2-2 zones, 1-3-1 zones, and 1-1-3 zones). This flexibility also gives the offense an important advantage of being able to use different schemes against different trap defenses. Having the opportunity of being able to use different sets and entries gives an offensive team two more distinct advantages: being able to take advantage of individual player's specific offensive strengths and/or being able to capitalize on individual opponent's weaknesses or that particular trap defense's general weaknesses.

With the flexibility and multiple options that this trap offense offers, this offense still remains a simple one for the offensive players to be able to learn and to be able to execute. Utilizing offensive breakdown drills allows each position player a method of being able to improve his own offensive skills and being able to perform them at a high degree of efficiency. The corners trap offense continually improves as a whole as each individual player improves his individual offensive skills, his knowledge and understanding of the offense, his confidence in performing the offense, and in the overall confidence of his teammates. All of these factors help make the overall offense more successful. The offense can become more and more efficient with its increasing use.

About the Author

John Kimble has 25 years of basketball coaching experience. Most recently, he served as the head basketball coach at Crestview (FL) High School for 10 years. During Kimble's tenure, the team averaged almost 18 wins each season (excluding his first year at the helm).

Kimble began his basketball coaching career as an assistant basketball coach at Lexington (IL) High School, serving as the head freshman coach, the head freshmansophomore coach, and the assistant varsity coach. During his one season at Lexington, the three squads each lost only two games, while amassing an overall 61-6 record. The varsity won the conference, regional, sectional, and super-sectional state tournament championships before losing in the state tournament's Elite Eight.

The following year, Kimble took the head basketball coaching position at Deland-Weldon (IL) High School, where the varsity accumulated a five-year record of 91-43 that included two regional championships, two regional runner-ups, and one sectional tournament runner-up. Next, he moved to Dunlap (IL) High School for five years. His overall 90-45 record at Dunlap included two regional runners-up, one regional, one sectional, and one super-sectional championship and a final second-place finish in the Illinois Class A State Tournament.

Kimble then moved to Florida, where he became an assistant basketball coach at Central Florida Community College in Ocala, Florida. The next year, he became the offensive coordinator in charge of the overall offense. For the next two years, he retained that offensive coordinator responsibility while also becoming an associate head coach, with a two-year record of 44-22. CFCC's overall record during Kimble's four years there was 73-58.

Kimble has worked 90 weeks of basketball camps and has spoken at several coaching clinics and camps. He also has had articles appear in publications such as *The Basketball Bulletin* of the *National Association of Basketball Coaches, The Scholastic Journal, Winning Hoops,* and *Basketball Sense,* and has contributed articles and diagrams to two different editions of the book *Coaching Basketball*.

Kimble is currently teaching several business classes at Crestview (FL) High School, still studying the game, and still writing basketball articles and books.